RUNNING YOUR

**SMALL BUSINESS
LIKE A PRO**

The More You Know, The Faster You Grow

WORKBOOK

ANDREW FRAZIER, MBA, CFA

This book is only available through the Small Business Pro University.

Small Business Pro University Press
Email: info@MySBPro.com
Website: www.SBProU.com

Cover Design and Layout: Andrew Frazier

Editing: Barry Cohen, John Larrier, and Hurley Fox

Library of Congress Control Number: xxxxxxxxxx

ISBN 978-1-970129-07-6

Printed in the United States of America

Other Books by the Author

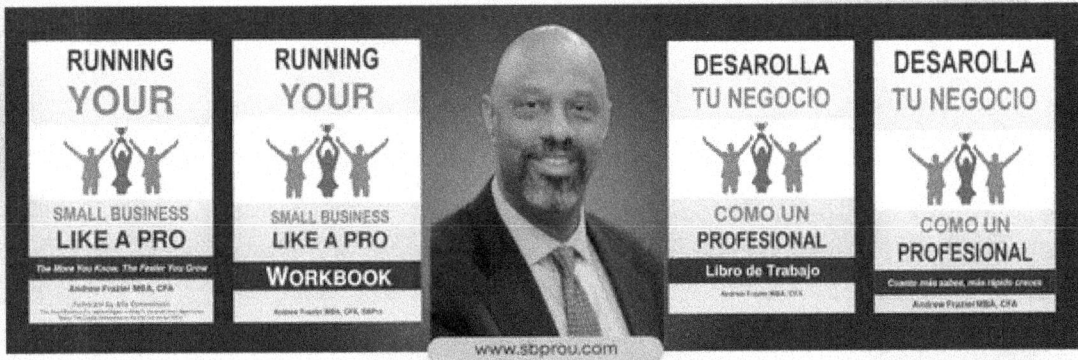

Coming Soon...

- 99 Proven Tips to Sell More, Maximize Profit, and Finance Growth
- Learning the Language of Business: What Every Business Owner Needs to Know
- Market Like A Drug Dealer and Win More Customers
- P.R.A.Y. for Financing: Get Your Business Financed Faster and Easier

Table of Contents

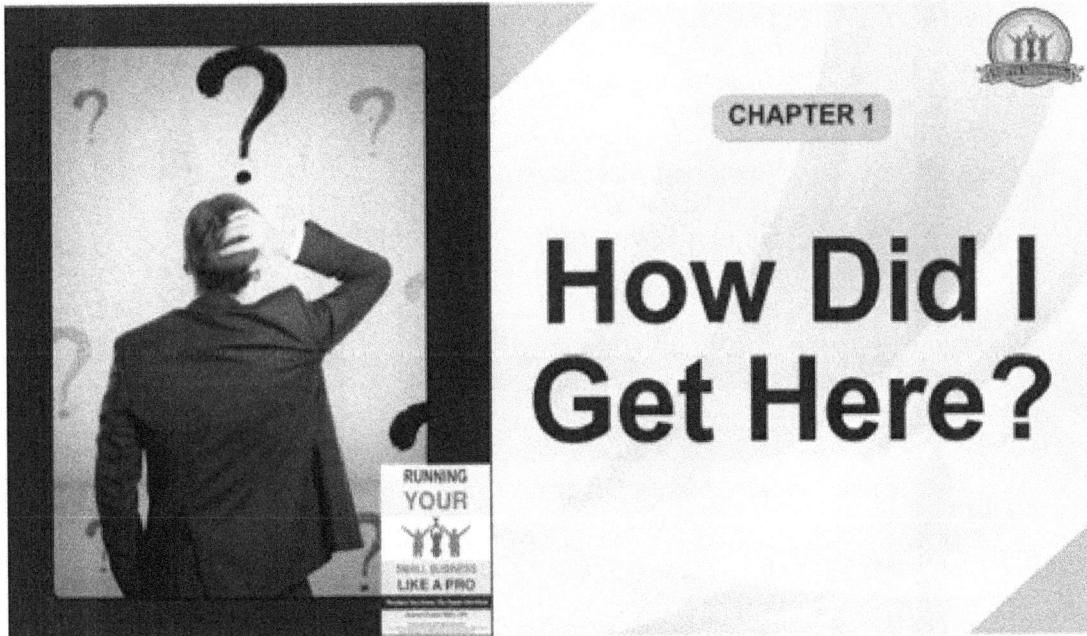

Chapter 1 – How Did I Get Here?

Chapter 1

How Did I Get Here?

'How did I get here' will help you think about and rethink your business purpose and growth plans. By completing these Activities, you will better understand how you ended up where you are. This chapter also outlines the "Critical Path" you must follow to create a sustainable business that can run without you. The path of working IN your business (product and service delivery), then ON your business (business model optimization), and finally ON THE FUTURE of your business (market expansion).

Key Concepts from this chapter:

Why do you want to be a business owner?
Importance of creating an enterprise
Setting and achieving your goals
Business planning
Growing your business knowledge
Increasing your capacity
Product and service delivery
Business model optimization
Market Expansion
SBPro Methodology

Exercises For This Chapter:

Business Rationale
Business Purpose
Business Types
Personal Growth Plan
Personal Knowledge Assessment

Activity 1: Business Rationale - Why are you in business?

SBPro® Business Rationale

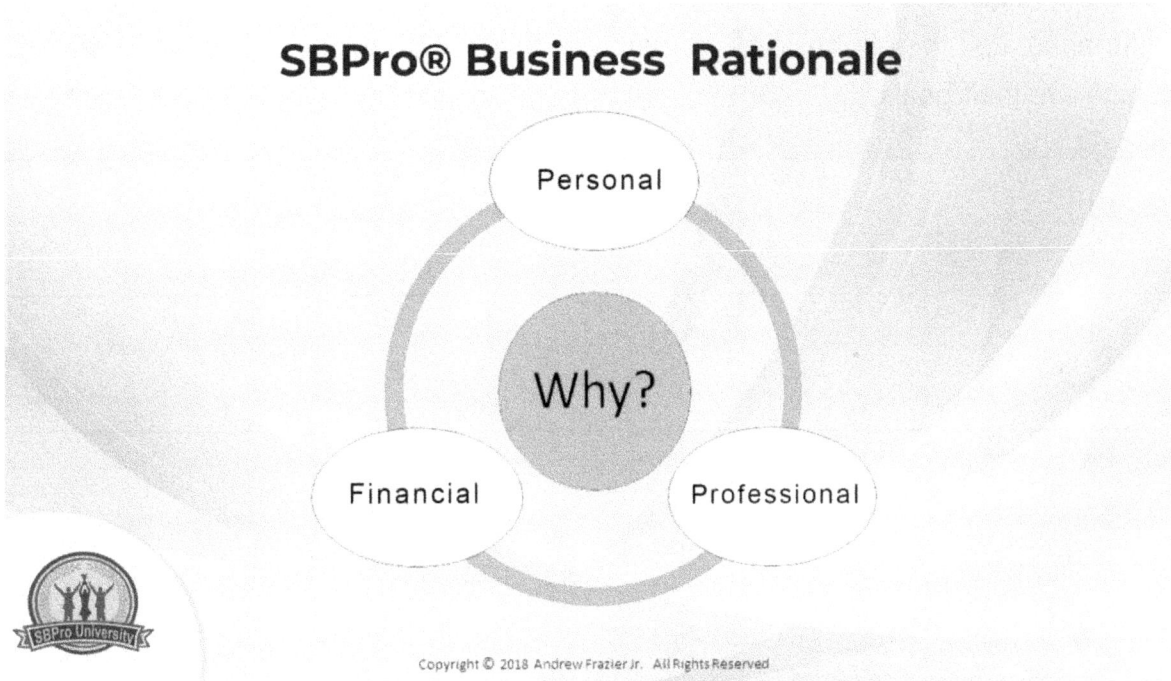

Copyright © 2018 Andrew Frazier Jr. All Rights Reserved

Please read the following options and check all that apply to you.

Freedom of being your boss		Self-actualization	
Flexibility to create your schedule		Make more personal connections	
More time for your family		To become wealthy	
To work remotely or travel		Multiple streams of income	
Creating long-term stability		To create passive income	
More significant impact to fill a void		To build something of your own	
Thought it would be cool		To push yourself	
Change of lifestyle		To learn from experience	
Reduce taxes		To get out of the rat race	
Ability to work with interesting, dynamic people and companies		Hiring people and creating jobs	
To make a difference		For your local community	
Family pressures		For your kids	
More interesting and fulfilling work		You can't work with others.	
Inability to get a job		You invented something	
To be free from constraints		To work with whom you want to	

In the space below, choose your top 3 selections and expand on why you chose these. For example, if you chose "To make a difference," explain why this was one of your top 3 AND how you hope to make a difference, i.e., to help business owners become more successful, allowing more business owners to achieve their goals.

1.	
2.	
3.	

Activity 2: Business Purpose

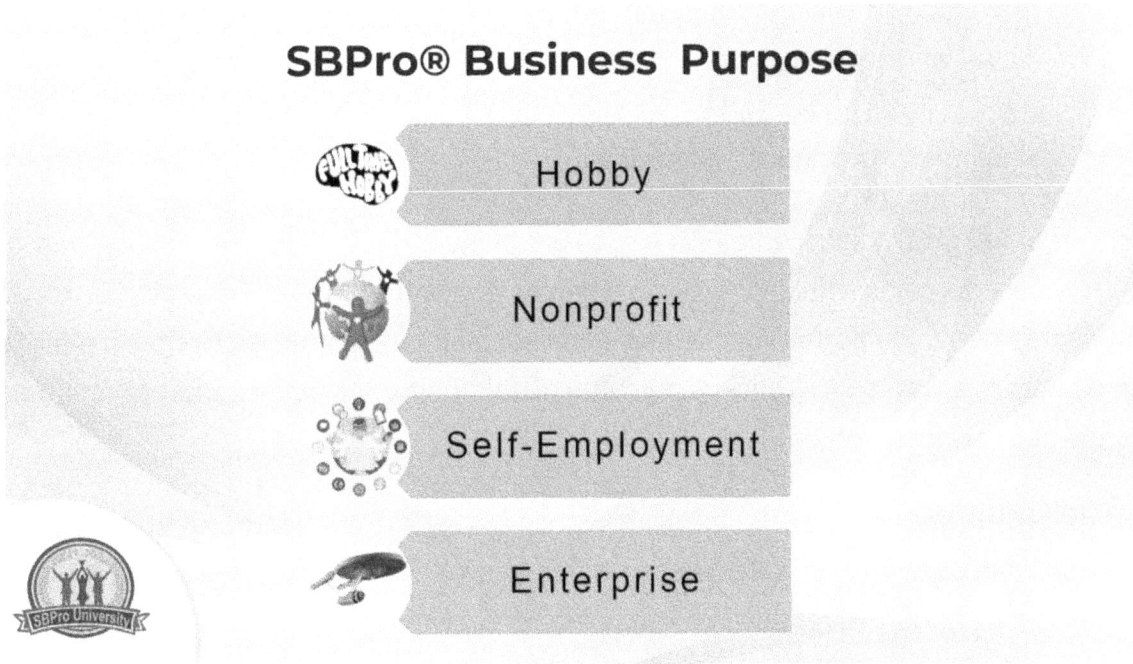

SBPro® Business Purpose

Hobby

Nonprofit

Self-Employment

Enterprise

Match the Business Purposes above to the correct definition below...

Business Purpose	Answer
1. Organized for accomplishing a mission rather than generating profit, and in which the organization's income is distributed for the greater good.	
2. An activity that you engage in "for sport or recreation, not to make a profit." Even if you earn occasional income from doing such an activity, the primary purpose is something other than making a profit.	
3. A business-oriented organization formed specifically so founders can show initiative and take risks to pursue expanding entrepreneurial endeavors for a profit.	
4. An individual earns income through conducting profitable operations from a trade or business that he or she directly operates.	

Activity 3: Your Business Types

Hobby—Pam always enjoyed drawing in her free time. She was very artistic and creative and soon started painting every day after work. Although she was not making money painting, she still enjoyed it. It helped her relax and pass the time. Before long, people started to ask if they could buy the paintings. Pam was excited and agreed to sell some of her paintings. She was thrilled to make a little money from something she previously did for free!

Non-profit – Michael grew frustrated by his city's lack of clean water. He knew many individuals who did not have access to clean drinking water, so he created a business plan to start a non-profit that could address this need. He began fundraising and reaching out to donors. He hired a few people to assist him with his mission to fix this issue. His business's primary focus was not to make money but to address the clean water problem.

Self-Employment—When Ryan no longer wanted to work for the large law firm he had worked for 25 years, he started his own business. Ryan was older and had enough clients to keep him busy and bring in more than enough revenue. He was able to continue saving for retirement and enjoyed working for himself. Ryan did not have the need or desire to hire employees.

Enterprise—As David's fishing business grew, he started hiring employees and building a foundation that could be scaled (no pun intended). After a few years of steady growth, David began hiring Senior-Level employees to expand his locations and remove himself from many day-to-day operations.

Using the information above, which type of business are you currently running, and which type do you want to be and why?

1. Currently running:

2. I want to be running:

Activity 4: Personal Growth Plan

SBPro® Growth Plan

Copyright © 2018 Andrew Frazier Jr. All Rights Reserved

What are your strengths, and where does your expertise lie?

What are your weaknesses, and where do you need assistance?

Activity 5: Personal Knowledge Assessment

Activity: Mark your level of knowledge for each

Subject Area	Level of Knowledge			
Sales	None	A Little	Proficient	Expert
Networking:				
Telemarketing:				
In-person sales:				
Online sales:				
Marketing				
Public Relations:				
Target Market:				
Campaigns:				
Plan:				
Management				
Strategy:				
Leadership				
Legal/HR:				
Time Management:				
Goal Setting:				
Operations:				
Business Law:				
Website / Social Media				
Website Building:				
Website SEO:				
LinkedIn:				
Instagram/Facebook:				
Twitter:				
YouTube:				
Yelp:				
Online Advertising:				
Computers / Technology				
Accounting software:				
Spreadsheets:				
Google Drive/Docs:				
ERP / MRP				
CRM System				
Finance:				
Bookkeeping:				
Financial Statements:				
Payroll:				
Projections:				
Taxes:				

Choose the three key areas you want to learn more about.

1.	
2.	
3.	

Which of these learning methods do you plan to employ?

YouTube Videos	Online Courses	Workshops/Seminars
Hiring Skilled Help	Reading Books	Info Interviews
Mastermind Groups	Trial & Error	Professional Organizations
One-on-One Coaching	Online Research	College Courses

SBPro® Critical Path

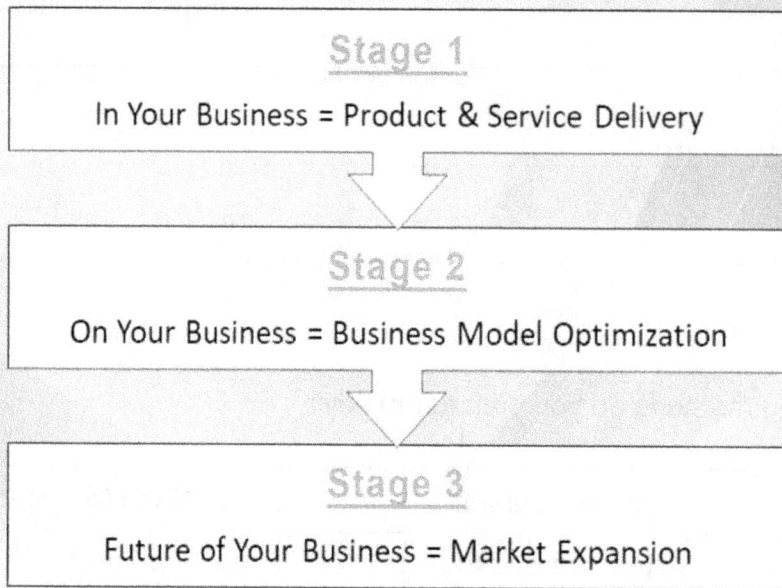

Stage 1

In Your Business = Product & Service Delivery

Stage 2

On Your Business = Business Model Optimization

Stage 3

Future of Your Business = Market Expansion

SBPro® Methodology

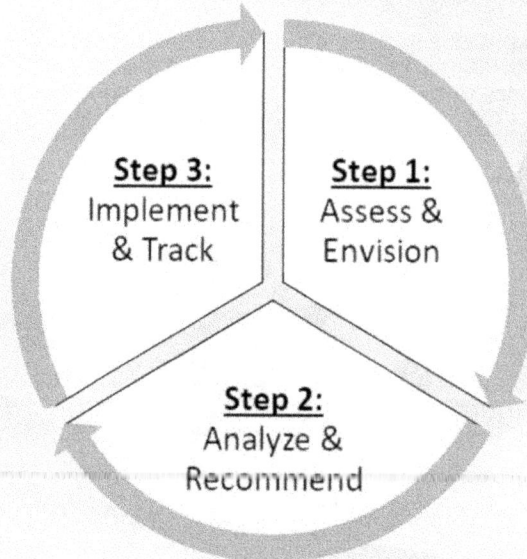

Step 3:
Implement
& Track

Step 1:
Assess &
Envision

Step 2:
Analyze &
Recommend

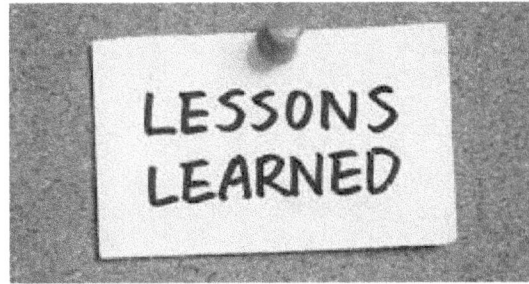

Key Learnings:

Chapter 1 - How Did I Get Here?

1) Consider why you are a small business owner and what benefits you seek.

2) Understand whether creating an enterprise is critical to achieving your goals.

3) Develop and continually update a plan for growing your business knowledge, your organization's capacity, and the markets you serve.

4) Follow the critical path of working IN your business (product and service delivery), then ON your business (business model optimization), and finally ON THE FUTURE of your business (market expansion).

5) Use the SBPro Methodology as your process for continual improvement.

Learn, Profit, and Grow!

www.SmallBusinessLikeAPro.com

SMALL BUSINESS
LIKE A PRO
The More You Know, The Faster You Grow

CHAPTER 2

The Most Important Job?

Chapter 2 – What is My Most Important Job?

Chapter 2

What is My Most Import Job?

Key Concepts from the Book

Marketing and selling
Training, practicing, and learning from other businesses
Narrow target market
Branding
Focusing on the customer

List of Activities

Who is most likely to buy from you?
Marketing budget
Building relationships
Strengths and weaknesses
Unique selling proposition
4-step commercial process
Ideation
Creating Your Pitch

3 Reasons to Market Like A Drug Dealer

Working with over 1,000 small business owners in many different industries, I have found that being able to market effectively is a significant challenge. Not necessarily because they do not want to, but because they may not understand how to do it. As part of my coaching, I tell my clients they need to market their business like a drug dealer. Skepticism is not uncommon, but people always find this activity valuable because it is a simple way to learn the three most important factors in marketing their small business more effectively.

Activity 1 - Don't Sell to Everyone (Target Market)

What are some reasons why finding the right target market is essential?

- Effectiveness and efficiency
- Higher conversion rate
- Lower customer acquisition cost
- Customers who value what you are offering
- Focus on value vs. price
- Limited dollars to invest
- Communicating more effectively
- To reduce the size of the battlefield
- Spending time focusing only on potential customers
- Save time and energy
- Get important feedback from those who are interested in your product

Activity 2 - Don't Overpay for Marketing (Budget)

Elections are won by focusing on the people who are most likely to vote, just like **business is won** by **focusing on** those who are **most likely to buy**.

Who Is Most Likely to Buy from You?

Needs, Wants, Desires	
Geography / Location(s)	
Industry / Nationality	
Number of Employees	
Decision Maker / Race	
Income / Revenue Range	
Age / Years in Business Range	
Relationship / Affinity	
Education / Hobbies	
Work / Job	

Many new business owners often spend too much money on marketing and advertising, putting their new business in a compromising position. It is easy to overspend on marketing, and costs can get out of control quickly. Make sure to plan and avoid wasting money on activities that will not position you to generate additional revenue.

Below is a quick budgeting Activity to help you estimate and plan your marketing expenses. Next to each expense, write down how much you plan on spending. Then, total these items to get your total budget. This number can be your startup or annual costs. We have provided rough numbers to help you. After you have completed the Activity, take a moment to reflect on whether this total amount is too high based on your revenue and other expenses.

Marketing Budget:

Business Cards	($10 - $150)	
Domain & Email	($10 - $350)	
Website	($0 - $20,000)	
Brochures	($0 - $500)	
Video	($0 - $10,000)	
Logo	($0 - $1,250)	
Photography	($0 - $750)	
Other:		
Other:		
Other:		
	TOTAL BUDGET	

Activity 3 - Make Friends (Relationships)

A business can run without doing many things, but marketing and selling are not one of them.

What are some ways that you can build relationships today?

1.
2.
3.
4.
5.
6.
7.
8.

From the list below, check if a skill is a **strength, neutral, or weakness**. Below, write how you can improve on one weakness AND use one strength to help your company grow.

Skill	Strength	Neutral	Weakness
Active Listening			
Small Talk			
Introduction by Friends			
Quick Follow Up			
Remember Key Dates			
Communication Skills			
Social Media Profiles			
Extending Yourself			
Empathy			
Storytelling			
Social Media Profiles			
Cold Calling			
Patience			
Commitment/Reliability			
Remembering Names			
Generosity			
Integrity			
Positive Outlook			

How can I improve one weakness?

How can I use one of my strengths to grow my company?

It is important to meet your clients where they are. For example, if you are selling a product for older women you would want to focus on different marketing areas than if you were selling a product for college aged males.

1. Media Consumption Habits (tv, radio, social media, online video)

2. Personal Relationships (friends, family, work, school, neighbors)

3. Activities (social, sports, family, organizations, causes, religion, gym, YMCA, etc.)

4. Shopping (online, malls, catalogue, boutique, flea market, street fairs, etc.)

5. Communication Style (phone, text, mail, fax, social media)

Why should people choose to buy from you?

What is your unique value/selling proposition?

1.	
2.	
3.	

The 60-second commercial

4 Step Commercial Process

Step 1: Create the Need - Use facts about customer needs, wants, or desires for your product and/or service to create an emotional connection. Potential customers want to know that you understand what they need. Using facts, you can identify their problems or challenges and demonstrate an understanding of their specific needs, wants, or desires. In the case of life insurance, few people walk around thinking about purchasing it. Then, how are insurance agents able to get people to buy? They use facts such as having the person think about what happens when one member of a couple dies. "Have you ever been to a wake where the family had to pass the hat to cover the costs of the funeral?" After hearing that information, the person will think about life insurance as something they may need.

List three facts, questions, or beliefs below that will show clients you understand their business needs and challenges.

1.
2.
3.

Step 2: **Introduce Your Solution** - Explain who you are and how you will address their challenge by explaining your solution and what differentiates you from the competition. For example, again, in the case of life insurance, the agent indicates, "As an independent agent, I offer life insurance policies from all the major companies, ensuring that people get the best products and pricing possible."

Below, list three reasons why you are different and how the **solution(s)** you offer to address the problems you mentioned in step one.

Why are you different?

1.

2.

3.

How will you help?

1.

2.

3.

Step 3: **Provide an Example**—Help the person visualize themselves benefiting from your solution through someone else's experience, such as, "My client, John Smith, passed away last month at the age of 42. During his family's time of need, I brought his wife, Mary, a check for $1 million to maintain their lifestyle and ensure that the kids, Lisa and Tommy, can still go to college."

Below are two examples of previous clients you have helped.

1.

2.

Step 4: **Strong Close with Soft Ask** – Open the door to start a conversation and develop a relationship with potential customers. For example, "While an unfortunate situation, think how much worse that would have been if John had not sat down with me and obtained the coverage he needed."

Below, provide TWO one-sentence "hooks" that can start a conversation with a potential customer. Use the example above as guidance.

1.
2.

Gauge their response to determine the next steps. If they ask questions or start a conversation about what you can do for them, they will move from being a prospect to a lead. However, those who do not are unlikely customers but potential referral sources.

Activity #7 - Ideation

Step 1: Below is a list of 3 facts that show you understand the clients' needs and problems.

Examples

a. Many small businesses with superior products and services lose because they are out-marketed by larger competitors.

b. Professionals are often afraid to market for fear that it makes them appear unprofessional.

c. Highly credentialed professionals often fail to achieve a high public profile.

Creating The Need

1.

2.

3.

Step 2: Below is a list of 3 reasons why you are different and at least three solutions you have to address the problems you mentioned in number one above.

Why are you different?

a. We bring a consumer products marketing approach to marketing professionals and practitioners.

b. We give tremendous one-on-one attention to clients.

c. We charge for our services on a predictable flat-rate basis.

Solutions:

a. We help unknown, first-time authors achieve perceived expert status.

b. We place professional practitioners in prestigious media environments.

c. We accelerate the expert status of professionals by making them thought leaders.

Differences

1.
2.
3.

Solutions

1.
2.
3.

Step 3: Below are two examples of previous clients you have helped.

Examples

1. By completing a makeover of her book and placing the author in prestigious media outlets, we helped Jane Doe's company attract new business opportunities. If Jane had tried to market the original version of her book on her own, she would never have achieved her current level of prominence so quickly.

2. After publishing his book, John Doe is now a sought-after speaker at numerous industry conferences and events. Had John not decided to go forward with his book, he would not have had the credibility to pursue investment for his next venture.

1.

2.

Step 4: Strong Close with Soft Ask – Open the door to start a conversation and develop a relationship with potential customers. For example, "While an unfortunate situation, think how much worse that would have been if John had not sat down with me and obtained the coverage he needed".

Below, provide TWO one-sentence "hooks" to start a conversation with a potential customer. Use the example above as guidance.

Examples

1. Is there any reason you wouldn't want to attract new business opportunities by being placed in prestigious media outlets?

2. Wouldn't being a sought-after speaker at numerous industry conferences and events help you achieve your goals faster and easier?

Soft Close "hooks"

1.

2.

Activity #8 – Creating Your Pitch

Example

How to change the conversation at a dinner party, restaurant, garden, grocery store…

Step 1: Create The Need

"This food or flower is incredible, and it wouldn't be possible without bees. Hopefully, they don't go extinct soon. Did you know they are disappearing at alarming rates due to the excessive use of pesticides in crops, and that the extinction of bees would mean the end of humanity?"

Now that the need has been established and the topic of conversation is where you want it to be, the solution (the product) can be pitched…

Step 2: Provide Your Solution

"To fight this decline, my business helps people save the bees and enjoy fresh honey. We bring two apiaries(beehives) to your backyard so that your gardens and flowers thrive, you have all the honey you want, and you're helping American agriculture, and the bees stay alive.

It is essential to provide an example of how your solution works so that they can imagine how it would benefit them.

Step 3: Give An Example

"For example, a farmer, one of our customers, purchased four beehives last year. He doubled his produce output, produced enough honey to sell in the marketplace, and has helped save the planet by saving over 100,000 bees."

Finally, you want to qualify whether they have an interest (a lead).

Step 4: Strong Close with A Soft Ask

Is there any reason why you wouldn't want to help save humanity by keeping bees while at the same time enhancing your garden and enjoying natural honey?

From here, you want to answer any questions they have and follow up if they are a lead.

Your Turn

Now it's time to pull everything together and write your 60-second commercial below…

Create the need…
Provide your solution…
Give an example…
Strong close with a soft ask…

LESSONS LEARNED

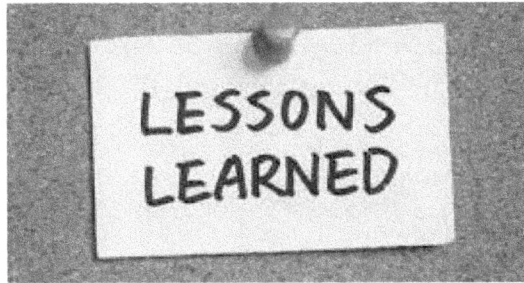

Chapter 2 - What is My Most Important Job?

1) Know that your most important job is to market and sell, which should be done for at least 2 hours daily.

2) It is essential to continually improve your skills by training, practicing, and learning from what other businesses do.

3) The smaller and more narrowly defined your target market, the more success you will have.

4) Branding is proactively working to create the image you want others to have of your business.

5) People are not purchasing what you are selling; they are buying what they believe you are selling does for them. Please focus on the customer and speak to their needs.

SBPro University

Learn, Profit, and Grow!

www.SmallBusinessLikeAPro.com

SMALL BUSINESS LIKE A PRO

The More You Know, The Faster You Grow

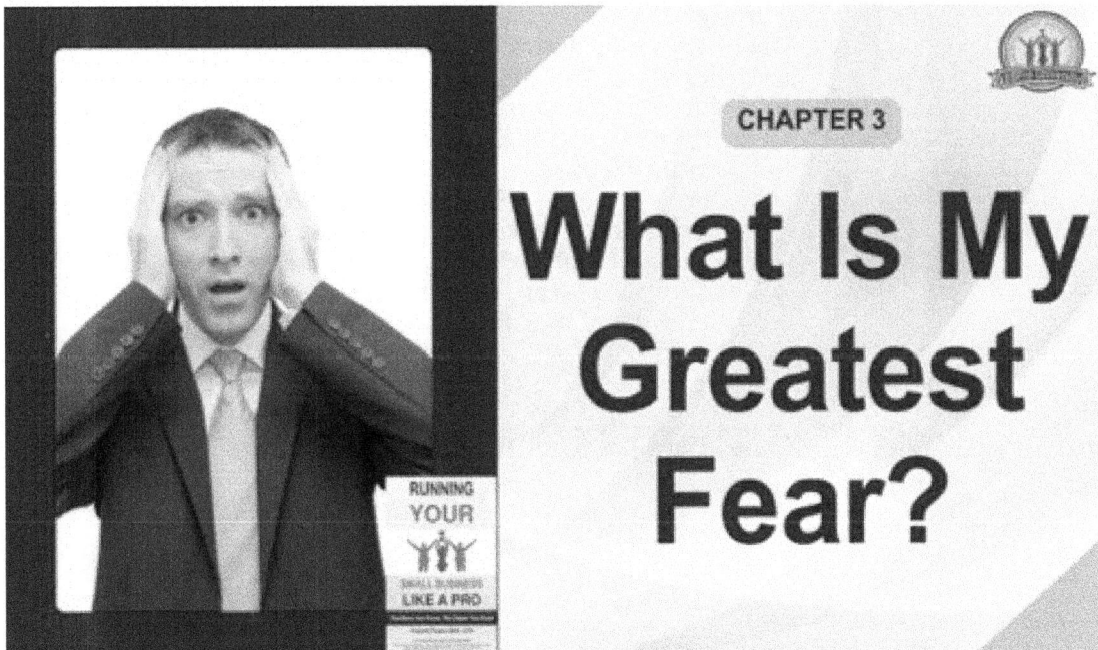

CHAPTER 3

What Is My Greatest Fear?

Chapter 3 – What Is My Greatest Fear?

Chapter 3

What is My Greatest Fear?

Key Concepts from the book

Understanding the numbers
Good decisions vs learning from bad decisions

List of Exercises:

Matching – Key Financial Terms
Matching – Financial Statements
Matching – Definitions
Matching – Business model
Multiple choice – Business categories
Formula fill-in
Multiple choice – Business Expenses
Income statement categorization
Balance Sheet categorization
Cash Flow statement categories
Matching – Cash flow statement

Activity 1: Key Financial Terms:

Activity 1: Match the following accounts with their corresponding accounting definitions:

Assets _____	1. The net amount of money being transferred into and out of a business, especially as affecting liquidity
Liabilities _____	2. The level of ownership or book value
Revenues _____	3. Anything of value that was purchased and is retained within the business
Equity _____	4. a company's legal and financial debts or obligations that arise during regular business operations
Expenses _____	5. Costs associated with running a business
Profit _____	6. Gross income generated from normal business operations with discounts and returns included
Cash flow _____	7. a financial gain, the difference between sales and expenses

Activity 2: Match the names and definitions of the key financial statements.

Income statement _____	a. net amount of cash and cash equivalents being transferred into and out of a business
Balance sheet _____	b. Tells how much money the business made by subtracting expenses (fixed and variable) from the revenue (sales). Also known as profit and loss.
Cash flow _____	c. A financial statement that reports a company's assets, liabilities, and shareholders' equity at a specific point in time.

Activity 3: Match the following accounts with their corresponding definitions.

Accounts Payable	_____	1. Value of on-hand raw materials, work-in-progress, and finished goods based on cost
Deprecation	_____	2. Expenses that have been paid in advance
Retained earnings	_____	3. Money owed to the company by customers
Accounts receivable	_____	4. Money owed by a company to its suppliers
Inventory	_____	5. A reduction in the value of an asset over time.
Notes payable	_____	6. Payments from investors in exchange for an entity's stock.
Prepaid expenses	_____	7. An agreement owed by a company to another person or business
Paid-in-capital	_____	8. The accumulated net income of the company that is retained within the company.

Activity 4: Match the key categories of the business model.

COGS	_____	a. business expenses that must be paid whether there are sales or not
Revenue	_____	b. total sales minus total expenses
Variable costs	_____	c. business expenses that have a direct relationship with sales
Fixed costs	_____	d. the financial gain after deducting the cost to deliver a business's products and services
Gross profit	_____	e. the book value of goods sold during a particular period
Net income	_____	f. gross income generated from customers minus discounts and returns

Activity 5: Classify words into the categories - asset (A), liability (L) or expense (E)

Cash	_____	Accounts Payable	_____
Utilities	_____	Wages Payable	_____
Equipment	_____	Rent	_____
Income Taxes Payable	_____	Notes Payable	_____
Company Car	_____	Company Building	_____
Accounts Receivable	_____	Supplies	_____
Interest Payable	_____	Savings Accounts	_____
Inventory	_____	Land	_____

Activity 6: Formula fill-in using the word bank below.

Cash Flow = _____ − _____

Profit = _____ − _____

Assets = _____ + _____

Word Bank
• Equity
• Cash outflows
• Expenses
• Sales
• Cash inflows
• Liabilities

Activity 7: When budgeting and finding essential numbers, knowing the difference between Fixed Costs and Variable Costs is critical. To give you some practice, we have listed some expenses every business has, and you need to put each expense into the proper category. Determine fixed "FC" or variable cost/COGS "VC."

Insurance	_____	Property Taxes	_____
Salaries	_____	Credit Card Fees	_____
Utilities	_____	Rent	_____
Raw Materials	_____	Commissions	_____
Interest Expense	_____	Production Employee Wages	_____

Activity 8: Income Statement Categorization

An Income Statement tells how much money the business made by subtracting expenses (fixed and variable) from revenues (sales). Also known as the Profit & Loss (P&L) or business model. In the exercise below fill in the Type column with the abbreviation of the corresponding statement section for each item in the word bank. This exercise will help you learn the parts of an Income Statement.

Income Statement		
Company Name: R on's Jewelry		
Date:		
Revenue:		
R	$	10,398.00
R	$	5,293.00
Total Revenue:	$	15,691.00
Cost of Goods Sold:		
CGS	$	2,387.00
CGS	$	1,783.00
CGS	$	290.00
Total Cost of Goods Sold:	$	4,460.00
Gross Profit (Loss):	$	11,231.00
Fixed Expenses		
FE	$	2,500.00
FE	$	250.00
FE	$	223.00
FE	$	80.00
TOTAL FIXED COSTS	$	3,053.00
NET PROFIT	$	8,178.00

Word Bank (write the corresponding section abbreviation next to each item)			
	TYPE		**TYPE**
Utilities		Shipping Costs	
Bracelet Supplies		Insurance	
Rent		Bracelet Sales	
Internet		Necklace Supplies	
Necklace Sales			

Activity 9: Balance Sheet Categorization

A Balance Sheet provides the financial position of the business at a single point in time, like a personal net worth statement. Financial statements make it much easier to both understand and manipulate the numbers. A lot of additional information about your business can be learned by analyzing the financial statements. For more information on the importance of the numbers and financial statements see Chapter 3 of Running Your Small Business Like a Pro. Complete the exercise at the bottom of the sheet.

Balance Sheet

Company Name:

Date:

Assets			Liabilities		
Current Assets			**Current Liabilities:**		
CA	$	100.00	CL	$	200.00
CA	$	5.00	CL	$	150.00
CA	$	100.00	CL	$	45.00
CA	$	50.00	Total Current Liabilities	$	395.00
CA	$	75.00			
Total Current Assets	$	330.00			
			Long Term Liabilities		
Fixed Assets			LTL	$	700.00
FA	$	2,000.00	LTL	$	1,000.00
FA	$	1,200.00	Total Long Term Liability	$	1,700.00
Total Fixed Assets	$	3,200.00			
			Equity		
			E	$	600.00
			E	$	835.00
			Total Equity	$	1,435.00
Total Assets	$	3,530.00	Total Liabilities & Equity	$	3,530.00

Word Bank (Write the corresponding section abbreviation next to each item)

Building & Equipment		Accounts Payable	
Loans		Retained Earnings	
Paid In Capital		Depreciation	
Mortgage		Inventory	
Accounts Receivable		Prepaid Expenses	
Unpaid Expenses		Notes Payable	
Cash		Deposits	

Activity 10: Cash Flow Statement Categories

Investing Cash Flow ____	1. The amount of cash a company has at the start of the fiscal period. This is equal to the cash balance from the previous fiscal period.
Ending Cash ____	2. Cash related to raising capital, dividends, and debt repayment, providing insight into how a company funds its operations and growth.
Operating Cash Flow ____	3. The difference between a company's total cash inflows and outflows over a specific period provides insight into its financial health and liquidity.
Net Cash Flow ____	4. The amount of cash or equivalent a company has at the end of a specific period.
Financing Cash Flow ____	5. Cash generated or spent on activities like buying or selling long-term assets, securities, or other companies.
Beginning Cash Flow ____	6. The cash a company generates from its core business activities.

Activity 11: Cash Flow Statement Activity Matching

Determine which cash flow activities are affected by the transactions below:

- Operating Cash Flow "O"

- Investing Cash Flow "I"

- Financing Cash Flow "F"

- Not a Cash Flow "N"

Loan from the Bank	____	Invoiced Sale	____
Inventory Purchase Cash	____	Equipment Purchase	____
Utility Payment	____	Rent	____
Raw Materials	____	Commissions	____
Interest on a Loan	____	Production Employee Wages	____
Purchase a Building	____	Stock Purchase	____
Loan Principal Payment	____	Cash Sale	____
Admin Employee Wages	____	Inventory Purchase Credit	____
Depreciation	____	Credit Card Purchase	____

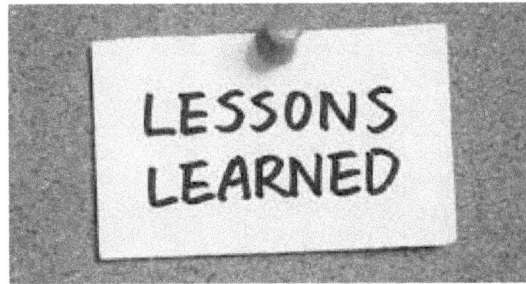

Key Learnings:

Chapter 3 - What is My Greatest Fear?

1) Doing the numbers is not as scary as it seems.

2) You can't understand your business if you don't understand the numbers

3) Without numbers, you end up working "IN" rather than "ON" your business

4) The numbers help you to plan more effectively and anticipate problems.

5) Waiting will only cost you more money (i.e., good decisions vs. learning from bad decisions).

Learn, Profit, and Grow!

www.SmallBusinessLikeAPro.com

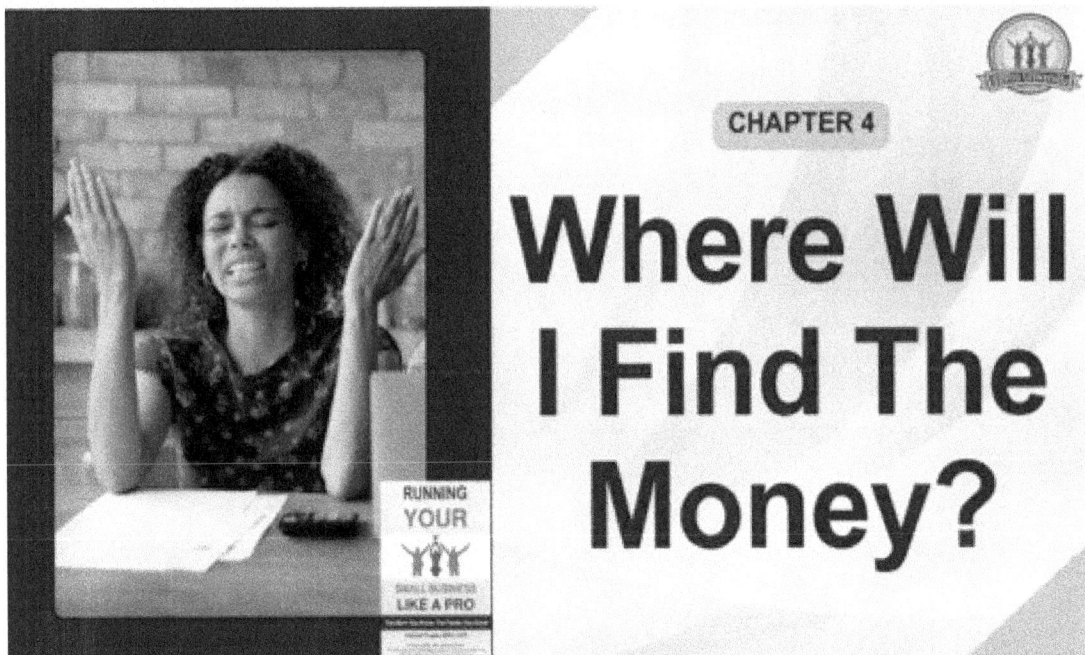

Chapter 4 – Where Will I Find the Money?

Chapter 4

Where Will I Find the Money?

Key Concepts from this chapter:

Personal credit score and report
Collateral
Filing taxes
Full disclosure and credibility

List of Exercises

True or false
Multiple choice – Personal Credit
Matching – Types of Investors
Matching – Financing Documents
True or False
Matching – Credit Terminology

Obtaining financing is not easy, and Chapter 4 is designed to educate you on the challenges and what you can do to increase your chances of securing financing. P.R.A.Y. for financing is a proven strategy for improving the likelihood and magnitude of funding for your business…

Prepare   Research   Assemble   Yield

Activity 1: True or False – USEFUL KNOWLEDGE ABOUT FINANCING

	T or F
1. Since the 2008 financial crisis, securing business financing has become significantly easier.	
2. The amount of documentation, planning, and preparedness needed for financing is much higher.	
3. Most small business owners seeking financing do not get it because they lack a viable business plan and/or the necessary cash flow.	
4. Knowledge about how your business works does not include knowing your business model.	
5. Crowd funding is an easy way to raise capital	
6. Financing your business with grants is the best strategy.	
7. A variable-rate loan is always better than a fixed-rate loan.	
8. The biggest reason for underestimating what is needed to start your business is not including working capital.	
9. It does not matter if your accountant knows whether you are seeking financing.	

10. If your start-up costs are $100,000, you most likely need to contribute a *minimum* of $25,000.	

Activity 2 - Personal Credit: To help you better understand credit scores and credit reports, complete the following multiple-choice Activity.

Knowing your credit score, understanding your credit report, and working to increase your credit score are critical to getting your business the funding it needs. If you do not know your score, visit www.freecreditreport.com, any of the credit bureaus' websites, or your bank, which most likely has a free credit report for you. Once you know your score, read through your credit report to understand what is positive and negative about it, and put together a plan to increase your score.

Question	Employers	Auto Lenders	Credit Card Issuers	Collections Agencies
Which group(s) cannot access your credit report without written permission?				

Understanding a Credit Report	Harm Score	Improve Score	Maintain Score
1. A lot of requests for new lines of credit will…			
2. Disputing inaccuracies on your credit report will…			
3. Getting a copy of your credit report will…			
4. Paying off a past due balance will…			
5. Not paying your bills on time will…			
6. Getting professional help will…			
7. Paying off debt will…			
8. Contacting your creditors will…			
9. Leaving credit accounts open with zero balance will…			

Activity 3: Investor Types

Matching different types of investors

Personal Investment _____	1. Best for loans of $10,000 or less, or up to $25,000 or $50,000. These lenders focus on businesses that cannot get traditional bank financing
Friends and Family _____	2. Best when working with larger companies and governmental institutions, who may take 45-60-90 days before they pay you on an invoice
Microlender _____	3. Private individuals and groups of people who have pooled their money and like to invest in promising startups and early-stage businesses
Cash-Flow Lenders _____	4. The first step in the financial process; no one will give you money without this
Trade Credit _____	5. Extremely difficult to obtain, and there are many strings attached
Factoring (AR & PO) _____	6. These lenders range from commercial / community/savings/investment/ merchant / private banks to credit unions
Traditional Banking _____	7. Will finance you based on the cash flow going into and out of your business
Angel Investors _____	8. A likely investment because they know or like you
Venture Capital (VC) _____	9. Generally, it requires that a business is profitable with a proven product or service and has the potential to grow significantly
Private Equity _____	10. Involves getting payment terms from your suppliers so that you do not have to pay them C.O.D.

Activity 4: Key Financing Documents

Matching – The documents that are required

Personal/business tax returns ____	1. A report that lists unpaid customer invoices and unused credit memos by date ranges
Year-to-date financial statements ____	2. a printed record of the balance in a bank account and the amounts that have been paid into it and withdrawn from it, issued periodically to the account holder.
Personal financial statements ____	3. a document setting out a business's future objectives and strategies for achieving them.
Accounts receivable aging report ____	4. gives you an overview of what your business owes for supplies, inventory, and services
Debt schedule ____	5. A form on which a business owner makes an annual statement of income and personal circumstances, used by the tax authorities to assess liability for tax
Business plan ____	6. The document(s) are filed initially with the appropriate State Authority, known as Articles of Incorporation or Certificate of Formation.
Driver's license ____	7. lays out all the debt a business has in a schedule based on its maturity, usually used by businesses to construct a cash flow analysis
Bank statements ____	8. A document or spreadsheet outlining an individual's financial position at a given point in time
Company formation documents ____	9. A document permitting a person to drive a motor vehicle.
Listing of equipment ____	10. A brief account of a person's education, qualifications, and previous experience
Accounts payable aging report ____	11. formal records of the financial activities and position of a business, person, or other entity for the full calendar year
Bio/resume/certifications ____	12. Inventory of all tagged equipment with equipment number, service description, capacity, dimension and size, weight, required power, PO number, reference P&ID numbers, as well as key summary information of those tagged equipment items

Activity 5 - After Submission (nothing else is needed)

	T / F
1. No further documentation is needed	
2. I cannot do any work while my documents are submitted	
3. Waiting is easy	
4. You will probably meet the person who approves your loan	

Activity 6: Matching - Credit terminology

Credit Limit	____	a. A financial number that indicates how likely you are to repay debt and make timely payments.
Credit Score	____	b. A record of your information, including payment habits, as reported by your creditors to a credit reporting agency. It serves as a financial reference when you apply for credit or other services
Credit Report	____	c. The maximum dollar amount you can borrow, or the maximum an account can show as an outstanding balance

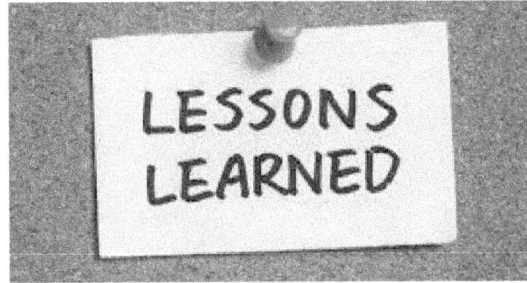

Chapter 4 - Where Will I Find the Money?

1) Your personal credit score and report are critical.

2) Having collateral is extremely helpful.

3) Your taxes must be filed to show you are making money.

4) No surprises – full disclosure is a must. It is better to declare something negative than to become a surprise later in the process. Credibility is one of the pillars for being able to obtain financing.

Learn, Profit, and Grow!

www.SmallBusinessLikeAPro.com

SMALL BUSINESS LIKE A PRO

The More You Know, The Faster You Grow

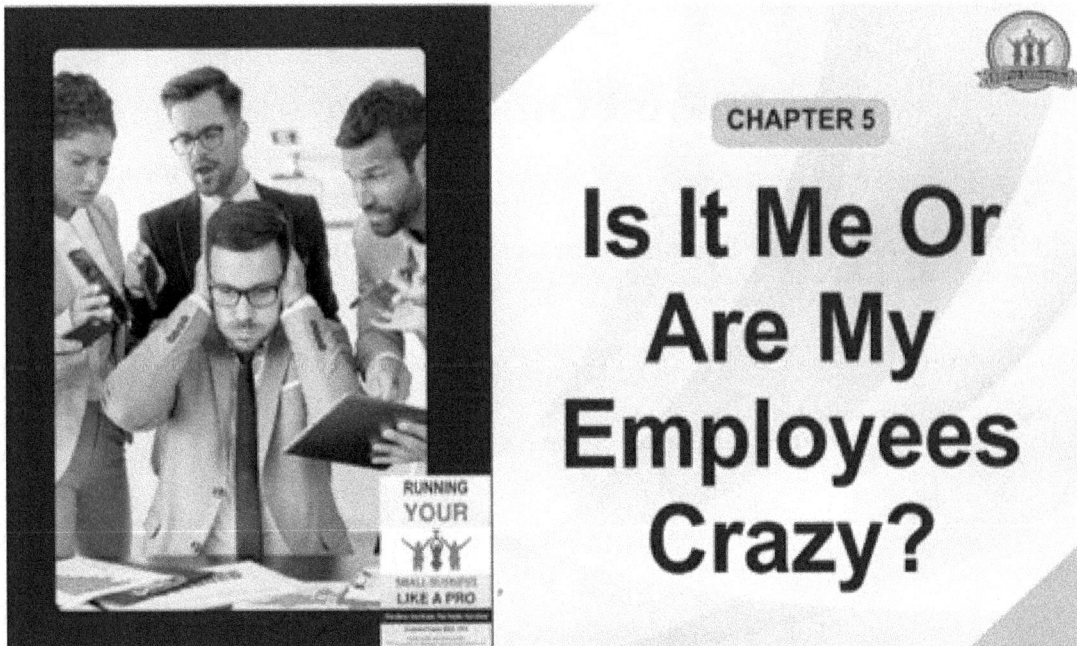

CHAPTER 5

Is It Me Or Are My Employees Crazy?

Chapter 5 – Is it Me or Are My Employees Crazy?

Chapter 5

Is It Me or Are My Employees Crazy?

As your organization grows, your primary role will shift from managing your organization to leading it. This is best done by setting an example, by setting policies, and by developing the best culture (environment) to achieve your goals. You cannot delegate all three tasks to someone else; they are critical in moving your organization forward. Since you have probably never done this, you will need outside help regarding coaching, consulting, and/or training. If you do this right, your role at the company will be more of a symbol, a communicator, and a facilitator instead of focusing on day-to-day business operations. *Now, this is important for moving from working **IN** your business to working **ON** your business and must be completed if you ever want to be able to spend most of your time working **ON THE FUTURE** of your business.*

SBPro® Critical Path

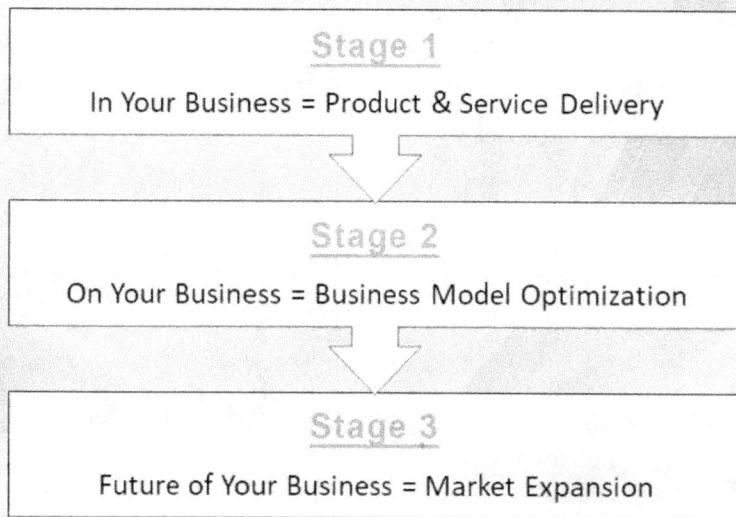

Stage 1
In Your Business = Product & Service Delivery

Stage 2
On Your Business = Business Model Optimization

Stage 3
Future of Your Business = Market Expansion

Copyright © 2018 Andrew Frazier Jr. All Rights Reserved

Key Concepts from the books

Hiring employees
Managing people
Being a supervisor and manager
Having control
Creating structure, processes, and systems

List of Exercises

Matching – Role description
Multiple choice – Role & tasks
True or false
Matching – Role description
Matching – Definitions

Questions to focus on:

What responsibilities will you have as your business grows?
What do you do vs what do your employees do?

Activity 1 - Business Structure

Match the four roles with their correct description.

Role		Description
Employee	_____	a. ensures that people do their jobs and that weekly goals are achieved. They also provide feedback on performance.
Supervisor	_____	b. a person responsible for running an organization; they run companies or government agencies and create plans to help their organizations grow.
Manager	_____	c. work to continually improve the business in terms of developing strategies and plans to increase sales and productivity, working through others rather than directly with everyone
Executive	_____	d. performs duties with proper care and diligence on daily tasks specified by the employer

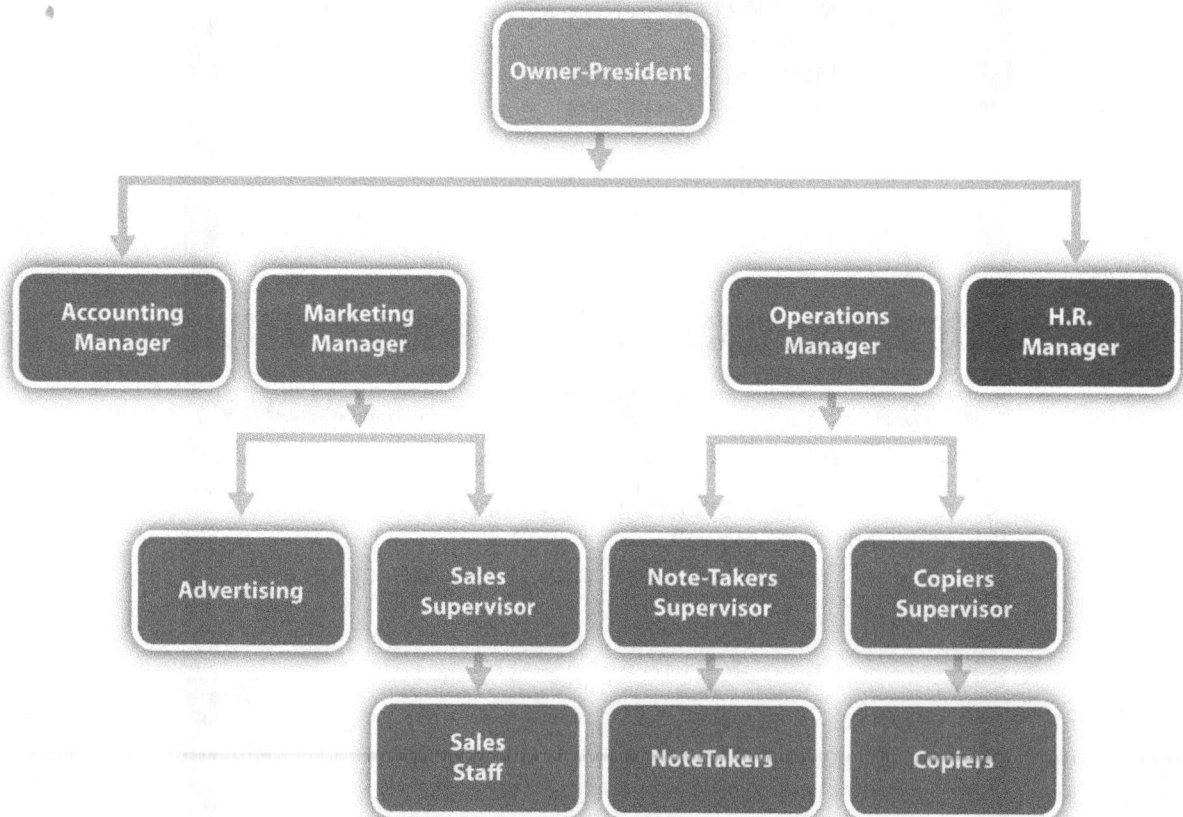

Business Structure - Activity 2

Assign the business tasks to the correct role.

Business Tasks	Employee	Supervisor	Manager	Executive
1. Whose job is it to set and help the team understand performance targets and goals?				
2. Whose duty is it to perform various responsibilities as they are instructed?				
3. Who directs and oversees an organization's financial and budgetary activities?				
4. Who is responsible for strategic planning, directing, and overseeing the operations and fiscal health of the organization?				
5. Who should oversee training and ensure that workers are properly trained for their specific roles?				

Activity 3 - Business Structure

Decide whether the following descriptions are True or False.

	T/F
It is easy to be both a good supervisor and an effective manager simultaneously.	
Managing, hiring, and dealing with people is the easiest responsibility of a small business owner.	
Organizational structure comes before processes, which come before systems are developed.	
Since you own the business, have control, and can make all the rules, you alone have the tools to create a better situation.	
Adding people to your small business will not have much impact.	

Activity 4 - Business Structure

Choose the best-fitting role to match the description.

Role Description	Employee	Supervisor	Manager	Executive
1. If I work at a hotel and handle the daily operations, including making sure there is enough inventory for meals, adequate staff, and ensuring customer satisfaction, I am a(n):				
2. I work for an ice cream shop, and I am the person who scoops the ice cream. This makes me a(n):				
3. If I create complete business plans for the attainment of goals and objectives, I am a(n):				
4. If my duties consist of managing workflow, organizing work groups, coaching employees, monitoring progress, enforcing rules, and ensuring quality compliance, this makes me a(n):				

Activity 5 – Business Structure (Systems, Processes & Procedures)

Match the terms with their definition.

Systems	____	1. a collection of linked tasks that find their end in the delivery of a service or product to a client
Procedures	____	2. a document that instructs workers on executing one or more activities of a business process
Rules	____	3. refers to the beliefs and behaviors that determine how a company's employees and management interact and handle outside business transactions
Processes	____	4. defines or constrains some aspect of business and generally resolves to either true or false
Culture	____	5. a collection of procedures, processes, methods, and/or courses of action designed to achieve a specific result.

Chapter 5 - Is It Me or Are My Employees Crazy?

1) Adding people inherently changes your organization, whether for the good or for the bad.

2) Managing, hiring, and dealing with people is one of the most challenging responsibilities of most small business owners.

3) It is difficult, if not nearly impossible, to be both a good supervisor and an effective manager simultaneously.

4) Since you own the business, have control, and can make all the rules, only you have the tools to create a better situation.

5) Creating a business's structure, processes, and systems is not necessarily easy or quick.

6) You must create an organizational structure before you can have processes, and you must have processes before you can develop systems.

Learn, Profit, and Grow!

www.SmallBusinessLikeAPro.com

Chapter 6 – Can I Get My Old Job Back?

Chapter 6

Can I Get My Old Job Back?

Key Concepts from the books

> Personal risk
> Getting paid
> Workload
> Business mixed with personal
> Commitment

List of Exercises:

> Entrepreneur vs. Employee
> Owning vs Working
> Business Ownership True/False
> Case Study – Making the Transition

Activity 1 – Entrepreneur vs. Employee

List the pros and cons of owning a business.

Topic:	
Pros	**Cons**

Activity 2 - Owning vs Working

Label the descriptions as either *"O" for owning* your business or *"W" for working* for someone else.

1. Create your work schedule.	
2. Complete any task commanded of you.	
3. Your personal, social, and financial life is more at risk	
4. You are "checked out" when you leave the office.	
5. Your output is directly proportional to the amount of work you put in.	
6. Possibility of being let go at any moment.	
7. Very little control.	
8. Become independent and fully responsible.	
9. Learn how to make do with a few resources.	
10. I struggle to balance work and free time.	

Activity 3 - Business Ownership True/False

	T / F
1. You will always be the first to get paid because you own the business.	
2. As a business owner, you will likely work harder than ever and make less money than expected.	
3. Initially, your personal credit carries more weight than the business credit.	
4. Personal health is a factor when considering starting your own business.	
5. A benefit of having W-2 income while starting a business is that banks prefer this when giving loans to new businesses.	
6. Your business life remains separate from your personal life.	
7. Having a business is like raising a child; it will take center stage in your life.	
8. Having the right insurance when starting a business is essential.	
9. Everybody pays you right on time.	
10. The government is lenient regarding late or unpaid sales and payroll taxes.	
11. If your business makes more money, *you* always make more money.	
12. There is a difference between being a baker and owning a bakery.	
13. Sometimes it may make sense to start your business while working another full-time or part-time job.	
14. Knowing about startup costs and fixed expenses in advance is critical.	
15. It is always better to obtain other sources of financing rather than using your own funds.	

16. People tend to leave companies, not people.	
17. As a business owner, it is not important if you know how to sell.	

Activity 4 – Case Study: Making the Transition

The following is a monthly budget and weekly schedule for Juan, an accountant currently working for a large firm. After reviewing the budget and schedule, you must complete a series of Activities.

Juan and his wife have two children (10 & 12) and live in the home they bought 5 years ago. Juan has been passed over for promotions for the past two years and often disagrees with his boss. Juan is also becoming frustrated with his lack of purpose. 18 months ago, Juan began saving to start his own business and has $10,000 in savings. Juan also paid off all other debt except for their home and cars, which have low interest rates and are almost paid off. Juan knows he can work from home and that three of his current clients will follow him wherever he goes. These three clients would bring Juan $50,000 a year.in business income

Juan's current monthly Budget:

Income from Twin Partners Accounting: $84,000 a year = $7,000 a month. Juan receives only $4,000 a month after taxes, health insurance, and the excellent 401k match program the firm offers. In addition to his salary, Juan also receives education reimbursement and PTO from his firm.

Juan's wife is an adjunct professor, and she makes $2,000 a month, bringing their family's income to $6,000 a month.

Part 1 – Review Juan's monthly expenses below and write next to each expense if it is a want or a need. What amount do you think Juan could get his necessary monthly payments down to?

Current monthly expenses:

Monthly Items	Expense	Want or Need	Revised Expenses
Mortgage	$1,800.00		
Car Payments	600.00		
Food:	950.00		
Utilities, Cell Phones & Cable	450.00		
Clothes	200.00		
Gas	200.00		
Toys	100.00		
Misc.:	200.00		
Savings:	100.00		
Total	**$6,500.00**		

Part 2 – List two things that Juan and his wife could do to increase their income if Juan started his own business.

1.	
2.	

Part 3 – Why would Juan need to make over $84,000 in his own business to retain his current standard of living?

Part 4 - Juan's Weekly Schedule

Monday to Friday	
6am	Wake up & Activity
7am	Take the kids to school.
8am – 5pm	Work
5pm – 8pm	Dinner with the family and time with the kids
8pm – 9pm	Chores
9pm – 10pm	Relax with wife
10pm - Sleep	Sleep

On the weekends, Juan spends catching up on house duties, playing with the kids and taking them to activities, seeing family and friends, having a date night with his wife, attending church on Sunday, reading, and watching movies and TV.

After reading Juan's weekly schedule, list at least three changes Juan might have to make if he left his job and started his own business.

1.
2.
3.

Chapter 6 - Can I Get My Old Job Back?

1) In a business, you take a lot of personal risk; you are the last to get paid, that is, if any money is left.

2) As a business owner, you will likely work harder than ever and make less money than expected.

3) Quitting or giving notice is not as easy as it seems because your business life is intertwined with your personal life, both socially and financially.

4) Having a business is like raising a child. It will take center stage in your life and become part of your identity.

Learn, Profit, and Grow!

www.SmallBusinessLikeAPro.com

SMALL BUSINESS LIKE A PRO
The More You Know, The Faster You Grow

CHAPTER 7

How Will I Ever Retire?

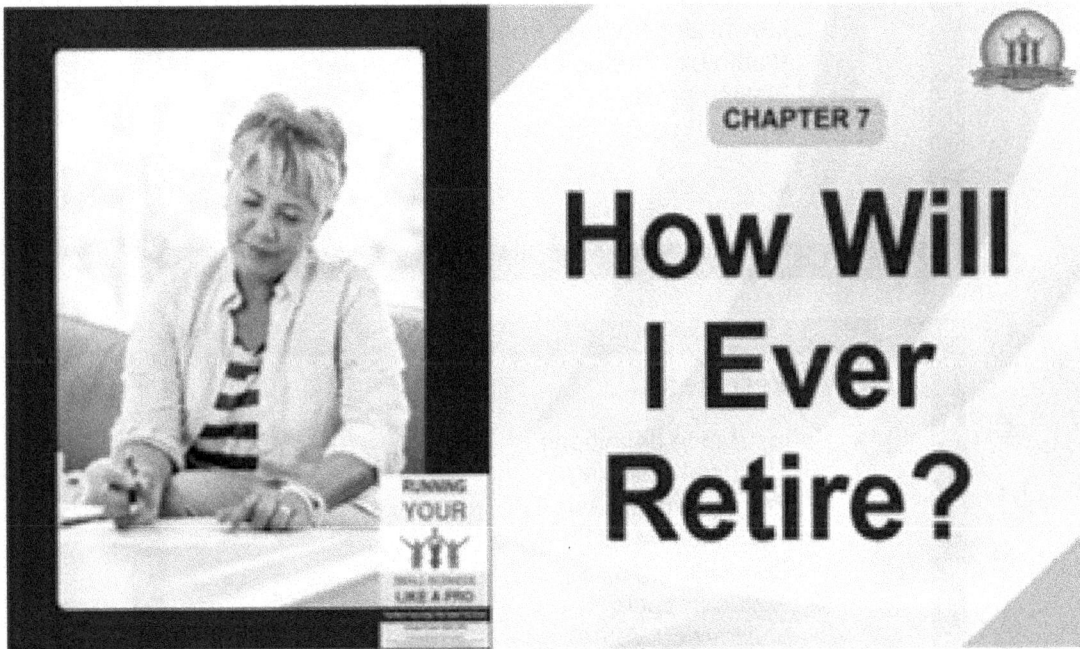

Chapter 7 – How Will I Ever Retire?

Chapter 7

How will I ever retire?

As the renowned educator Steven Covey, author of *The Seven Habits of Highly Effective People,* said, "Whatever you do, it is important to begin with the end in mind. When starting a business, you should think about your exit strategy." In the words of Michael Gerber, author of *eMyth*, "An entrepreneur's job is to figure out how he/she is going to get **_out_** of his or her business."

Key concepts from the book

> Entrepreneurial duties
> Retirement strategies
> Insurance
> Maximizing value of your business
> Viable exit strategies
> Making profits
> Obtaining a Builder Score

List of Exercises:

> Insurance definitions
> Financial Planning
> Permanent vs Term Life Insurance
> Insurance Facts
> Risk Mitigation
> Value Impacts
> Maximizing Value
> Increasing Value

Activity 1 - Insurance Definitions

Matching (Insurance) – Match the definition with the corresponding insurance term.

Permanent Insurance _____	1. A life insurance policy with Guaranteed Premiums and a Guaranteed Death Benefit. However, it has higher Premiums because of the guarantees.
Whole Life _____	2. The coverage amount stated in the policy contract is a key factor in determining premiums
Universal Life _____	3. An umbrella term for life insurance plans that build cash value and do not expire.
Variable Life _____	4. a person or entity who will receive the payout from a life *insurance* policy when the insured passes away.
Death Benefit _____	5. Life insurance that provides coverage at a fixed rate of payments for a limited period, the relevant term
Term Life Insurance _____	6. The policy has a cash value account, which is invested in several sub-accounts available within the policy.
Beneficiary _____	7. An insurance policy provision that adds benefits to or amends the terms of a basic insurance policy.
Face Value _____	8. The portion of an insurance policy that earns interest and may be available for the insured to withdraw or borrow against in case of an emergency.
Riders _____	9. The dollar amount that the policy owner's beneficiaries will receive upon the passing of the insured

Cash Value _____	10. Under the terms of the policy, the excess premium payments above the current cost of insurance are credited to the cash value of the policy, earning interest every month

Activity 2 - Financial Planning

Matching – Financial planning tools

Social Security	_____	a. A type of insurance benefit that provides some compensation or income replacement for non-job-related injuries or illnesses that render the insured unable to work for less than 6 months.
401k	_____	b. The combined portfolio holdings of stocks, bonds, or other assets. Each investor owns shares, which represent a part of these holdings.
Profit Sharing Plan	_____	c. A way to personally save for retirement outside of work that gives you tax advantages.
Annuity	_____	d. an insurance policy that protects an employee from loss of income if he or she cannot work due to illness, injury, or accident for more than 6 months.
Traditional IRA	_____	e. a legal agreement between two people before they are married that can cover a wide variety of issues centered on property rights and assets
Long Term Disability	_____	f. a federal insurance program that provides benefits to retired people and those who are unemployed or disabled
Major Medical Insurance	_____	g. insurance coverage that gives the insured extra liability coverage to help pay costs that exceed their general liability or other liability policy limits.
Short-Term Disability	_____	h. A defined contribution plan that lets companies help employees save for retirement
Prenuptial Agreement	_____	i. A qualified retirement plan that allows eligible employees of a company to save and invest for their retirement on a tax-deferred basis
Mutual Fund	_____	j. hospital, surgical, and medical insurance that provides comprehensive benefits as defined in the state where the contract will be delivered.

Umbrella Policy	_____	k. a fixed sum of money paid to someone each year, typically for a fixed period or the rest of their life

Activity 3 – Term vs Permanent Life Insurance

List the Pros & Cons between Permanent and Term Life Insurance

PROS of Permanent Life Insurance	CONS of Permanent Life Insurance

PROS of Term Life Insurance	CONS of Term Life Insurance

Activity 4 – Insurance Facts

Name the type of insurance each fact represents.

Insurance Facts	Term	Variable	Whole Life	Permanent	Universal
1. The simplest and cheapest type of coverage.					
2. This type of policy is also called "ordinary life" or "straight life".					
3. Offers only a pure death benefit with no cash value buildup.					
4. Invests the cash value that accumulates into variable mutual fund subaccounts that invest in stocks, bonds, cash, and real estate.					
5. This is one of the most popular forms of cash-value life insurance in the marketplace today and has three basic subcategories.					
6. Contains an account that accumulates cash value on a tax-deferred basis, and at least a portion of this money can usually be accessed at any time with no tax consequences and be used for any purpose.					
7. It only remains in force for a predetermined time, such as 10 or 20 years.					
8. Pays the policy owner dividends periodically, such as quarterly or					

annually, based on a guaranteed rate of interest.					

Activity 5 – Divorce Mitigation

Which of the following is not a recommended strategy for business owners to protect themselves and their assets in case of divorce?

1.	Review your options for establishing a buy-sell agreement, corporation, LLC, or a living trust to restrict ownership and ownership transfer.
2.	Revise your partnership agreement to require that the other partners have the option to buy out the interests of the divorced partner and his or her spouse.
3.	Carefully establish, fund, and manage your business with separate assets.
4.	Avoid co-mingling your business assets/accounts/expenses with personal assets/accounts/costs.
5.	Build up your company enough to the point that you are satisfied, and then try to sell.
6.	Pay yourself a market-rate salary.
7.	If a business is at issue in the divorce, a value must be placed on it. Agree on a number you both can live with. Then consider how to distribute it to your spouse by cash payment, by an offset against other assets you will waive, or with installment payments.

Activity 6 - Value Impacts

In the activity below, choose how each action will impact business value.

	Increases	Decreases	It Depends
1. Reducing reliance on a single customer.			
2. Focusing only on revenue.			
3. Increasing reliance on a single employee.			
4. Increasing reliance on a single supplier.			
5. Focusing on selling less stuff to more people.			
6. Creating recurring revenue.			
7. Moving your business to a better location with physical characteristics that are difficult to replicate.			
8. Having a customer that amounts to more than 20% of your revenue.			
9. Creating a unique product or service that is difficult to replicate.			
10. Not having audited statements.			
11. Creating predictable customer conversion rates.			
12. Having all the knowledge and power of the business in the hands of the owner.			
13. Not having a platform for customers to review products and services.			
14. Increasing profits.			
15. Developing a brand.			

Activity 7 - Value Maximization

Select True or False.

To maximize business value and avoid overestimating your business's value, you should...	T / F
1. Separate yourself from emotional attachment to the business.	
2. Set up your business so it is reliant on you.	
3. Sell hard assets like real estate.	
4. Understand how business valuation works.	
5. Develop relationships with potential buyers over time.	
6. Show income and profitability.	
7. Maintain a constant business size without scaling up.	
8. Develop a strong and recognizable brand that drives repeat business.	

Activity 8 – Increasing Value

Read the brief description of the business below and list three potential ways in which the company's value could be increased.

Due to age and health issues, a 65-year-old doctor wants to sell his business and retire early. He is the only doctor in practice, and during the past few years, the practice has declined because he has been working less. His advertising and marketing have not changed in 20 years, and he is currently leasing his office space in a remote part of town. While he has a long list of happy clients, his business is only valued at $100,000 when he was expecting $1MM.

What are three things he could do to increase his business's value?

1.

2.

3.

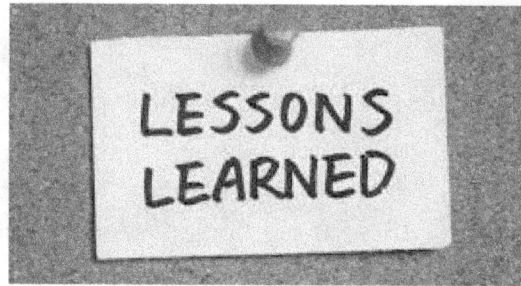

Chapter 7 - How will I ever retire?

1) An entrepreneur's job is to determine how he or she will get out of his or her business.

2) As a business owner, you are 100% responsible for figuring out and implementing a retirement strategy.

3) Prepare for retirement early by purchasing permanent life insurance, paying social security taxes, setting up a retirement plan, obtaining disability insurance, and staying married.

4) Focus on maximizing the value of your business and developing a viable exit strategy. Start at least five years before you might want to sell.

5) Profits, not sales, drive your company's value. A range of 2 - 4 times profits plus assets minus liabilities provides a general indication of value.

6) Obtain a Value Builder Score to see how your company is rated on the eight key business drivers. Visit https://valuebuilder.com/for-business-owners/

Learn, Profit, and Grow!

www.SmallBusinessLikeAPro.com

SMALL BUSINESS LIKE A PRO

The More You Know, The Faster You Grow

SBPro® Critical Path

Stage 1
In Your Business = Product & Service Delivery

Stage 2
On Your Business = Business Model Optimization

Stage 3
Future of Your Business = Market Expansion

CHAPTER 8

Running Your Business Like A Pro

Chapters 8, 9, 10, and 11 - This is How You Do It!

Activity 1 - True/False Questions

Questions	T/F
1. It is easier for a business owner to assess their own business objectively without external help.	
2. A business assessment should focus only on financial performance.	
3. Knowing your starting point and destination is critical for business success.	
4. Envisioning should include short-term, medium-term, and long-term goals.	
5. Creating a vision means drafting a simple vision statement.	
6. Financial analysis is optional when planning business growth.	
7. To develop an optimized business model, you must know your gross and net profits.	
8. Marketing analysis includes studying your competition.	
9. Fixed costs have no impact on business profitability.	
10. Implementation plans must define roles and responsibilities.	
11. Tracking performance is optional if you trust your employees.	
12. All initiatives should be rolled out simultaneously to save time.	
13. Measurement and tracking must include both qualitative and quantitative data.	
14. The SBPro Methodology is a one-time process.	

Activity 2 – Multiple Choice Questions

1. According to the workbook, which aspect is NOT essential when envisioning your business?
    - o A) Number of locations
    - o B) Revenue and profit goals
    - o C) Color schemes of your office
    - o D) Organizational structure

2. Why is external input often required during an assessment?
    - o A) To outsource responsibility
    - o B) To provide a more objective perspective
    - o C) To save money
    - o D) To create marketing materials

3. When should you reevaluate your vision?
    - o A) Only at the end of a decade
    - o B) Annually
    - o C) Every month
    - o D) Every week

4. Which is NOT a way to optimize your variable costs?
    - o A) Negotiate with suppliers
    - o B) Hire more managers
    - o C) Outsource non-core services
    - o D) Increase productivity

5. When creating recommendations, how many key initiatives should you focus on?
    - o A) 1 to 3
    - o B) 5 to 7
    - o C) 8 to 10
    - o D) As many as possible

6. Which of these is NOT part of successful implementation?
   - o A) Clear communication
   - o B) Defined responsibilities
   - o C) No need for measurements
   - o D) Organizational alignment

7. What is the final phase of the SBPro Methodology?
   - o A) Analysis
   - o B) Implementation & Tracking
   - o C) Assessment
   - o D) Branding

8. What kind of mindset should you maintain when tracking results?
   - o A) Passive
   - o B) Reactive
   - o C) Proactive
   - o D) Defensive

Activity #3 – Questions for Reflection

What are the most significant brutal truths you faced during your business assessment?

_____

_____

_____

_____

_____

_____

_____

Which recommendation will have the most significant impact if fully implemented?

_____

_____

_____

_____

_____

_____

_____

How can you ensure consistency in tracking your business's performance?

_____

_____

_____

_____

_____

_____

_____

_____

Chapter 8 -

1) Every business needs a defined process to move it forward.

2) The critical path to a successful entrepreneurial journey is working IN your business, then working ON your business, and finally working ON your business's future.

3) Most small business owners never get to work ON their business because they don't understand how or why.

4) You need to assess your business's current state, analyze its needs for future growth, and develop and implement a growth plan using SBPro Methodology.

5) SBPro Methodology Steps: Assessment and Envisioning, Analysis and Recommendations, Implementation and Tracking.

6) Consider hiring outside consultants to help you through this process.

Chapter 9

1) It is not easy to assess yourself accurately - get help.
2) The SBPro Assessment is a powerful tool that is easy to use.
3) Envisioning your business - you must see it before you can do it.

Chapter 10

1) Analysis helps you optimize the strategies used to achieve your goals
2) Always use the business model as part of your analysis
3) Focus on no more than three recommendations at a time

Chapter 11

1) Analysis helps you optimize the strategies used to achieve your goals
2) Always use the business model as part of your analysis
3) Focus on no more than three recommendations at a time

Answer Key

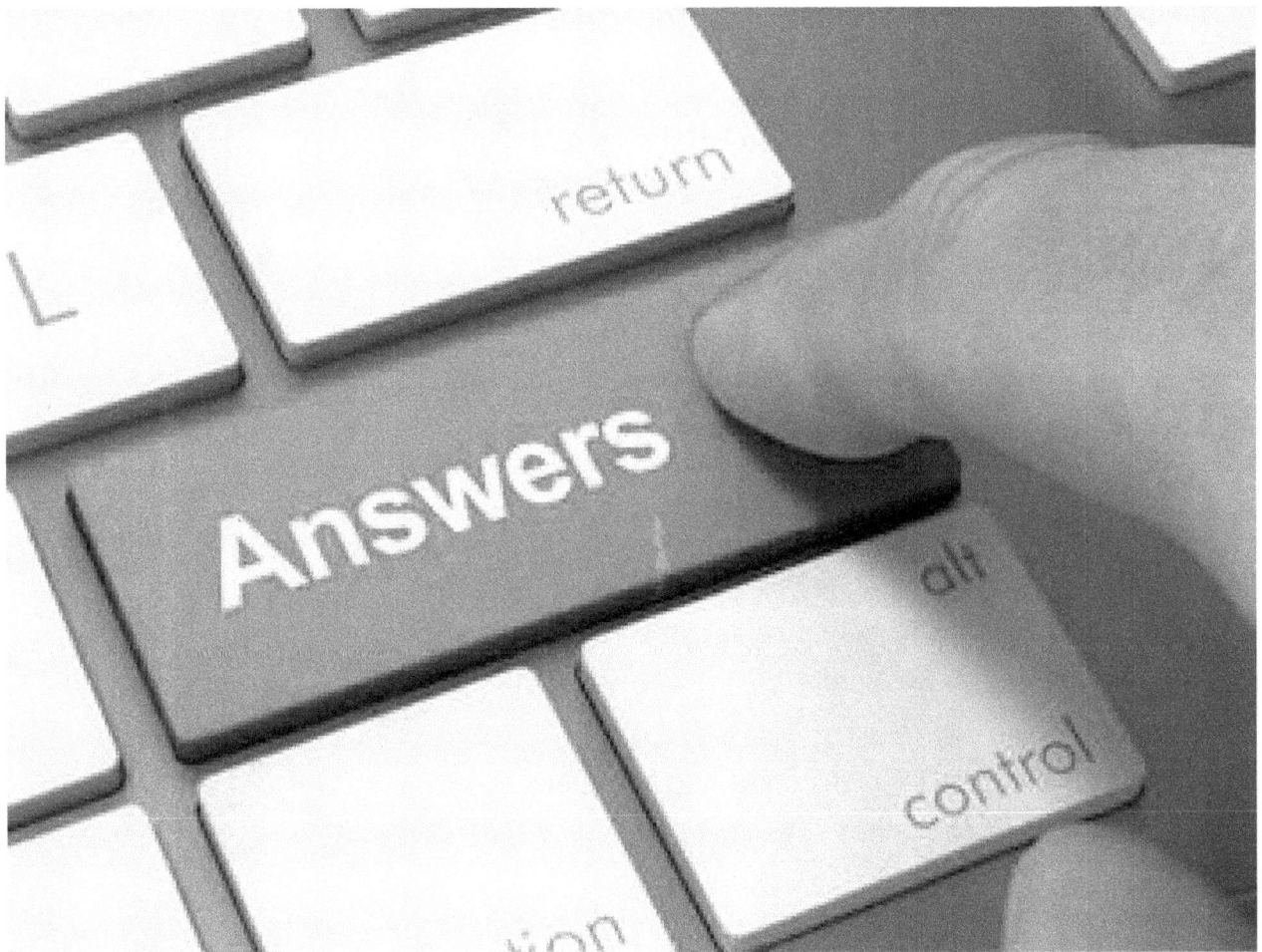

CHAPTER 1 - ANSWER KEY

'How did I get here' will help you think about and rethink your business purpose and growth plans. By completing these activities, you will better understand how you ended up where you are. This chapter also outlines the "Critical Path" you must follow to create a sustainable business that can run without you. The path of working IN your business (product and service delivery), then ON your business (business model optimization), and finally ON THE FUTURE of your business (market expansion).

Activity 1: Business Purpose

Match the Business Purposes above to the correct definition below...

Business Purpose	Answer
Organized for accomplishing a mission rather than generating profit, and in which the organization's income is distributed for the greater good.	**Nonprofit**
You engage in an activity "for sport or recreation, not to make a profit." Even if you earn occasional income from doing such an activity, the primary purpose is something other than making a profit.	**Hobby**
A business-oriented organization formed specifically so founders can show initiative and take risks to pursue expanding entrepreneurial endeavors for a profit.	**Enterprise**
An individual earns income through conducting profitable operations from a trade or business directly operating.	**Self-Employment**

CHAPTER 3 - ANSWER KEY

Activity 1: Match the following terms with their corresponding definitions:

Assets __3__	1. The net amount of money being transferred into and out of a business, especially as affecting liquidity
Liabilities __4__	2. The amount of net income left over for the business after it has paid out dividends to its shareholders
Revenues __6__	3. Anything of value purchased and retained in the business.
Equity __2__	4. an obligation to or something that you *owe* somebody else. A company's legal and financial debts or obligations that arise during business operations
Expenses __5__	5. Any cost a company purchases or spends money on
Profit __7__	6. Income generated from normal business operations included discounts and deductions for returned merchandise
Cash flow __1__	7. a financial gain, especially the difference between the amount earned and spent in buying, operating, or producing something.

Activity 2: Match the names and definitions of the key financial statements

Income statement __b__	a. Net amount of cash and cash equivalents being transferred into and out of a business
Balance sheet __c__	b. Tells how much money the business made by subtracting expenses (fixed and variable) from the revenue (sales). Also known as profit and loss.
Cash flow __a__	c. A financial statement that reports on a company's assets, liabilities, and shareholders' equity at a specific point in time

Activity 3: Matching

Accounts Payable __4__	1. A complete list of items such as property, goods in stock, or the contents of a building or business
Deprecation __5__	2. Expenses that have been paid in advance
Retained earnings __8__	3. Money owed to the company
Accounts receivable __3__	4. money owed by a company to its creditors
Inventory __1__	5. A reduction in the value of an asset with time, due to wear and tear.
Notes payable __7__	6. Payments from investors in exchange for an entity's stock.
Prepaid expenses __2__	7. An agreement owed by a company to another person or business
Paid-in-capital __6__	8. The accumulated net income of the corporation that the corporation retains at a particular point in time

Activity 4: Business Model matching

COGS __e__	a. business costs, such as rent, are constant regardless of the quantity of goods or services produced.
Sales __f__	b. income generated from normal business operations, and included discounts and deductions for returned merchandise
Variable costs __c__	c. a cost that varies with the level of output
Fixed costs __a__	d. the profit a company makes after deducting the costs associated with making and selling its products or the costs associated with providing its services
Gross profit __d__	e. the carrying value of goods sold during a particular period
Net income __b__	f. refers to any transaction where money or value is exchanged for the ownership of a good or entitlement to a service

Activity 5: Classify words into the categories - asset (A), liability (L) or expense (E)

Cash	___a____	Accounts Payable	__l____
Utilities	___e____	Wages Payable	___l____
Equipment	___a____	Rent	___e____
Income Taxes Payable	___l____	Notes Payable	___l____
Company Car	___a____	Company Building	___a____
Accounts Receivable	___a____	Supplies	___a____
Interest Payable	___l____	Savings Accounts	___a____
Inventory	___a____	Land	___a____

Activity 6: Formula fill-in

Cash Flow = ____cash inflows_____ – __cash outflows_____

Profit = ___sales_____ – ____expenses_____

Assets = ___liabilities_____ + _____equity_____

Word Bank
• Equity
• Cash outflows
• Expenses
• Sales
• Cash inflows
• Liabilities

Activity 7: When budgeting and finding essential numbers, knowing the difference between Fixed Costs and Variable Costs is critical. To give you some practice, we have listed some expenses every business has, and you need to put each expense into the proper category. Determine fixed "FC" or variable cost/COGS "VC"

Insurance	__FC__	Property Taxes	__FC__
Salaries	__FC__	Credit Card Fees	__VC__
Utilities	__FC__	Rent	__FC__
Raw Materials	__VC__	Commissions	__VC__
Interest Expense	__FC__	Production Employee Wages	__VC__

Activity 8 – Income Statement

An Income Statement tells how much money the business made by subtracting expenses (fixed and variable) from revenues (sales). Also known as the Profit & Loss (P&L) or business model. In the exercise below fill in the Type column with the abbreviation of the corresponding statement section for each item in the word bank. This exercise will help you learn the parts of an Income Statement.

Income Statement

Company Name: Ron's Jewelry

Date:

Revenue:

Type	Amount	
R	$ 10,398.00	
R	$ 5,293.00	
Total Revenue:		$ 15,691.00

Cost of Goods Sold:

Type	Amount	
CGS	$ 2,387.00	
CGS	$ 1,783.00	
CGS	$ 290.00	
Total Cost of Goods Sold:		$ 4,460.00
Gross Profit (Loss):		$ 11,231.00

Fixed Expenses

Type	Amount	
FE	$ 2,500.00	
FE	$ 250.00	
FE	$ 223.00	
FE	$ 80.00	
TOTAL FIXED COSTS		$ 3,053.00
NET PROFIT		$ 8,178.00

Word Bank (write the corresponding section abbreviation next to each item)

Item	TYPE	Item	TYPE
Utilities	FE	Shipping Costs	CGS
Bracelet Supplies	CGS	Insurance	FE
Rent	FE	Bracelet Sales	R
Internet	FE	Necklace Supplies	CGS
Necklace Sales	R		

Activity 9 – Balance Sheet

A Balance Sheet provides the financial position of the business at a single point in time, like a personal net worth statement. Financial statements make it much easier to both understand and manipulate the numbers. A lot of additional information about your business can be learned by analyzing the financial statements. For more information on the importance of the numbers and financial statements see Chapter 3 of Running Your Small Business Like a Pro. Complete the exercise at the bottom of the sheet.

Balance Sheet

Company Name:

Date:

Assets		Liabilities	
Current Assets		**Current Liabilities:**	
CA	$ 100.00	CL	$ 200.00
CA	$ 5.00	CL	$ 150.00
CA	$ 100.00	CL	$ 45.00
CA	$ 50.00	Total Current Liabilities	$ 395.00
CA	$ 75.00		
Total Current Assets	$ 330.00		
		Long Term Liabilities	
Fixed Assets		LTL	$ 700.00
FA	$ 2,000.00	LTL	$ 1,000.00
FA	$ 1,200.00	Total Long Term Liability	$ 1,700.00
Total Fixed Assets	$ 3,200.00		
		Equity	
		E	$ 600.00
		E	$ 835.00
		Total Equity	$ 1,435.00
Total Assets	$ 3,530.00	Total Liabilities & Equity	$ 3,530.00

Word Bank (Write the corresponding section abbreviation next to each item)			
Building & Equipment	FA	Accounts Payable	CL
Loans	LTL	Retained Earnings	E
Paid In Capital	E	Depreciation	FA
Mortgage	LTL	Inventory	CA
Accounts Receivable	CA	Prepaid Expenses	CA
Unpaid Expenses	CL	Notes Payable	CL
Cash	CA	Deposits	CA

Activity 10: Cash Flow Statement Categories

Investing Cash Flow _5__	1) The amount of cash a company has at the start of the fiscal period. This is equal to the cash balance from the previous fiscal period.
Ending Cash _4__	2) Cash related to raising capital, dividends, and debt repayment, providing insight into how a company funds its operations and growth.
Operating Cash Flow _6__	3) The difference between a company's total cash inflows and outflows over a specific period provides insight into its financial health and liquidity.
Net Cash Flow _3__	4) The amount of cash or equivalent a company has at the end of a specific period.
Financing Cash Flow _2__	5) Cash generated or spent on activities like buying or selling long-term assets, securities, or other companies.
Beginning Cash Flow _1__	6) The cash a company generates from its core business activities.

Activity 11: Cash Flow Statement Activity Matching

Operating **"O"** - Investing **"I"** - Financing **"F"** - Not a Cash Flow **"N"**

Loan from the Bank	_F__	Invoiced Sale	_N_
Inventory Purchase Cash	_O__	Equipment Purchase	_I__
Utility Payment	_O__	Rent	_O_
Raw Materials	_O__	Commissions	_O_
Interest on a Loan	_O__	Production Employee Wages	_O_
Purchase a Building	_I__	Stock Purchase	_F__
Loan Principal Payment	_F__	Cash Sale	_O__
Admin Employee Wages Paid	_O__	Inventory Purchase Credit	_N__
Depreciation	_N__	Credit Card Purchase	_N__

CHAPTER 4 - ANSWER KEY

Activity 1: True or False

	T or F
1. Since the financial crisis of 2008, it has become much easier to get any business financing.	F
2. The amount of documentation, planning, and preparedness needed for financing is much higher than before.	T
3. Most small business owners seeking financing do not get it because they do not know how much they need; they do not have a viable business plan, and/or they do not have the necessary cash flow.	T
4. Knowledge about how your business works does not include knowing your business model.	F
5. Crowdfunding is an easy way to raise significant amounts of capital	F
6. Financing your business with grants is the best strategy	F
7. A variable loan rate is always better than a fixed one.	F
8. The biggest reason for underestimating what is needed to start your business is not including enough working capital.	T
9. It does not matter if your accountant knows whether you are seeking financing.	F
10. If your start-up costs are $100,000, you most likely need to contribute a *minimum cash injection* of $25,000 for SBA funding.	F

Activity 2 – Personal Credit

To help you better understand credit scores and credit reports, complete the following multiple-choice Activities.

Question	Employers	Auto Lenders	Credit Card Issuers	Collections Agencies
Which group(s) cannot access your credit report without written permission?	X	X	X	

Understanding a Credit Report	Harm Score	Improve Score	Maintain Score
1. A lot of requests for new lines of credit will…	X		
2. Disputing inaccuracies on your credit report will…		X	
3. Getting a copy of your credit report will…			X
4. Paying off a past due balance will…		X	
5. Not paying your bills on time will…	X		
6. Getting professional help will…		X	
7. Paying off debt will…		X	
8. Contacting your creditors will…			X
9. Leaving credit accounts open will…	X		

Activity 3: Matching different types of investors

Personal Investment	_4_	1. Best for loans of $10,000 or less, or up to $25,000 or $50,000. These lenders focus on businesses that cannot get traditional bank financing
Friends and Family	_8_	2. Best when working with larger companies and governmental institutions, which may take 45-60-90 days before they pay you on an invoice
Microlender	_1_	3. Private individuals and groups of people who have pooled their money and like to invest in promising startups and early-stage businesses
Cash-Flow Lenders	_7_	4. The first step in the financial process: no one will give you money without this
Trade Credit	_10_	5. Extremely difficult to obtain, and there are many strings attached
Factoring (AR & PO)	_2_	6. These lenders range from Commercial/community/savings/investment/ merchant / private banks to credit unions
Traditional Banking	_6_	7. Will finance you based on the cash flow going into and out of your business
Angel Investors	_3_	8. A likely investment because they know or like you
Venture Capital (VC)	_5_	9. Generally, it requires that a business is profitable with a proven product or service and has the potential to grow significantly
Private Equity	_9_	10. Involves getting payment terms from your suppliers so that you do not have to pay them C.O.D.

Activity 4: Matching – the documents that are needed

Personal/business tax returns _5__	1. A report that lists unpaid customer invoices and unused credit memos by date ranges
Year-to-date financial statements _11__	2. A printed record of the balance in a bank account and the amounts paid into it and withdrawn from it, issued periodically to the account holder.
Personal financial statements _8__	3. A document setting out a business's future objectives and strategies for achieving them.
Accounts receivable aging report _1__	4. gives you an overview of what your business owes for supplies, inventory, and services
Debt schedule _7__	5. A form on which a business owner makes an annual statement of income and personal circumstances, used by authorities to assess liability.
Business plan _3__	6. The document(s) originally filed with the appropriate State Authority, commonly known as Articles of Incorporation or Certificate of Formation.
Driver's license _9__	7. lays out all the debt a business has in a schedule based on its maturity, usually used by businesses to construct a cash flow analysis
Bank statements _2__	8. A document or spreadsheet outlining an individual's financial position at a given point in time
Company formation documents _6__	9. A document permitting a person to drive a motor vehicle.
Listing of equipment _12__	10. A brief account of a person's education, qualifications, and previous experience
Accounts Payable aging report _4__	11. Formal records of the financial activities and position of a business, person, or other entity for the full calendar year
Bio/resume/certifications _10__	12. Inventory of equipment with number, service description, capacity, dimension and size, weight, required power, PO number, reference P&ID numbers, as well as key summary information of those tagged equipment items

Activity 5: After Submission of the financing package

	T/F
1. No further documentation is needed	F
2. I cannot do any work while my documents are submitted	F
3. Waiting is easy	F
4. You will probably meet the person who approves your loan	F

Activity 6: Matching - Credit terminology

Credit Limit	__C__	1. A financial number that indicates how likely you are to repay debt and make timely payments.
Credit Score	__A__	2. A record of your information, including payment habits, as reported by your creditors to a credit reporting agency. It serves as a financial reference when you apply for credit or other services
Credit Report	__B__	3. The maximum dollar amount you can borrow, or the maximum an account can show as an outstanding balance

CHAPTER 5 - ANSWER KEY

Activity 1: Match the four roles with their correct description.

Employee _D_	a. makes sure that the work gets done and ensures that your employees are doing their jobs; must be tough to deliver bad news, and to provide feedback to employees about their performance
Supervisor _A_	b. a person responsible for running an organization; they run companies or government agencies and create plans to help their organizations grow.
Manager _C_	c. be a leader, empower people, and inspire people to do their best; work on the business in terms of developing strategies and plans that consist of ways to increase sales and productivity; work through the supervisors rather than directly with all the employees
Executive _B_	d. performs duties with proper care and diligence specified by the employer

Activity 2: Assign the business tasks to the correct role.

Business Tasks	Employee	Supervisor	Manager	Executive
Whose job is it to set and help the team understand performance targets and goals?			X	
Whose duty is it to perform various responsibilities as they are instructed?	X			
Who directs and oversees an organization's financial and budgetary activities?			X	
Who is responsible for strategic planning, directing, and overseeing the organization's fiscal health?				X
Who should oversee training or ensure workers are properly trained for their specific roles?		X		

Activity 3: Decide whether the following descriptions are True or False

	T/F
It is easy to be both a good supervisor and an effective manager simultaneously.	F
Managing, hiring, and dealing with people is the easiest responsibility of a small business owner.	F
Organizational structure comes before processes, which come before developing systems.	T
Since you own the business, have control, and can make all the rules, only you have the tools to create a better situation.	T
Adding people to your business will not have much impact.	F

Business Structure Activity 4: Choose the best-fitting role to match the description.

Business Tasks	Employee	Supervisor	Manager	Executive
1. If I work at a hotel and handle the daily operations, including making sure there is enough inventory for meals, adequate staff, and ensuring customer satisfaction, I am a(n):			X	
2. I work for an ice cream shop, and I am the person who scoops the ice cream. This makes me a(n):	X			
3. If I create complete business plans for the attainment of goals and objectives, I am a(n):				X
4. If my duties consist of managing workflow, organizing work groups, coaching employees, monitoring progress, enforcing rules, and ensuring quality compliance, this makes me a(n):		X		

Activity 5: Match the terms with their definition

Systems	_5_	1. A collection of linked tasks for achieving a consistent outcome
Procedures	_2_	2. A document that instructs workers on executing one or more activities of a business process
Rules	_4_	3. refers to the beliefs and behaviors that determine how a company's employees and management interact and handle outside business transactions
Processes	_1_	4. defines or constrains some aspect of business and generally resolves to either true or false
Culture	_3_	5. A collection of procedures, processes, methods, or courses of action designed to achieve a specific result.

CHAPTER 6 - ANSWER KEY

Activity 1: Label the descriptions as either *"O" for owning* your own business or *"W" working* for someone else.

1. Create your work schedule.	O
2. Complete any task commanded of you.	W
3. Your personal, social, and financial life is more at risk	O
4. You are "checked out" when you leave the office.	W
5. Your output is directly proportional to the amount of work you put in.	O
6. Possibility of being let go at any moment.	W
7. Very little control.	W
8. Become independent and fully responsible.	O
9. Learn how to make do with few resources.	O
10. Struggle to separate work and personal identity.	O

Activity 2: True or False

	T / F
Because you own your own business, you are always the first to get paid.	F
As a business owner, you are most likely to work harder than ever and make less money than expected.	T
Your personal credit carries more weight than your business credit.	T
Personal health is a factor when thinking about starting your own business.	T
A benefit of having a W-2 income while starting a business is that banks prefer this when giving loans to new businesses.	T
Your business life remains separate from your personal life.	F
Having a business is like raising a child; it will take center stage in your life.	T
Having the right insurance when starting a business is important.	T
Everybody pays you right on time.	F
The government is lenient regarding late or unpaid sales tax.	F
If your business makes more money, *you* always make more money.	F
There is a difference between being a baker and owning a bakery.	T
Sometimes, it may make sense to start your business while working another full-time or part-time job.	T
It is critical to know startup costs and fixed expenses in advance.	T
It is always better to obtain funding from other sources rather than using your own money.	F
People tend to leave companies, not people.	F
As a business owner, it is not important if you know how to sell.	F

CHAPTER 7 - ANSWER KEY

Activity 1: Matching (Insurance)

Permanent Life Insurance	__3___	1)	A life insurance policy with Guaranteed Premiums and a Guaranteed Death Benefit. However, it has higher Premiums because of the guarantees.
Whole Life	__1___	2)	The coverage amount stated in the policy contract is a key factor in determining premiums.
Universal Life	__10__	3)	An umbrella term for life insurance plans that build cash value and do not expire.
Variable Life	__6___	4)	A person or entity who will receive the payout from a life *insurance* policy when the insured dies.
Permanent Death Benefit	__9__	5)	Life insurance that provides coverage at a fixed rate of payments for a limited period, the relevant term.
Term Life Insurance	__5___	6)	The policy has a cash value account, which is invested in several sub-accounts available within the policy.
Beneficiary	__4___	7)	An insurance policy provision that adds benefits to or amends the terms of a basic insurance policy.
Face Value	__2___	8)	The portion of an insurance policy that earns interest and may be available for the insured to withdraw or borrow against in case of an emergency.
Riders	__7___	9)	The dollar amount that the policy owner's beneficiaries will receive when the insured passes
Cash Value	__8___	10)	Under the terms of the policy, the excess premium payments above the current cost of insurance are credited to the cash value of the policy, earning interest every month

Activity 2: Matching – Other insurance/planning tools

Social Security ___f___	a) a type of insurance benefit that provides some compensation or income replacement for non-job-related injuries or illnesses that render the insured unable to work for less than six months.
401k ___i___	b) the combined portfolio holdings of stocks, bonds, or other assets. Each investor owns shares, which represent a part of these holdings.
Profit Sharing Plan ___h___	c) a way to personally save for retirement that gives you tax advantages.
Annuity ___k___	d) an insurance policy that protects an employee from loss of income if he or she is unable to work due to illness, injury, or accident for more than 6 months
Traditional IRA ___c___	e) a legal agreement between two people before they are married that can cover a wide variety of issues centered on property rights and assets
Long Term Disability ___d___	f) a federal insurance program that provides benefits to retired people and those who are unemployed or disabled
Major Medical Insurance ___j___	g) insurance coverage that gives the insured extra liability coverage to help pay costs that exceed their general liability or other liability policy limits.
Short-Term Disability ___a___	h) a defined contribution plan that lets companies help employees save for retirement
Prenuptial Agreement ___e___	i) a qualified retirement plan that allows eligible employees of a company to save and invest for their retirement on a tax-deferred basis

Mutual Fund	__b__	j)	hospital, surgical, and medical insurance that provides comprehensive benefits as defined in the state where the contract will be delivered.
Umbrella Policy	__g__	k)	a fixed sum of money paid to someone for a specific period or for the rest of their life

Activity 3: List of Pros & Cons between Permanent and Term Life Insurance

PROS of Permanent	CONS of Permanent
Coverage can last your entire lifetime.	More expensive
Your cost of insurance does not go up during your lifetime.	More complex insurance options. (Whole, Variable, and Universal)
There is an investment and savings component with a buildup of cash value.	It is more difficult to qualify for permanent insurance.

PROS of Term	CONS of Term
Less expensive	Coverage only lasts for a specified period, and you must renew at a higher rate.
Easier to qualify for term insurance	Price increases significantly when renewed at an older age.
It allows you to get more coverage for specific times when needed (i.e., family needs and debt)	May not be able to renew if health status changes significantly
Increase coverage easily and inexpensively over a specific period.	No cash value
Able to choose from several different coverage periods. (5, 10, 20, and 30-year terms)	

Activity 4: Name the type of insurance each fact represents.

Insurance Facts	Term	Variable	Whole Life	Permanent	Universal
1. The simplest and cheapest type of coverage.	X				
2. This type of policy is also called "ordinary life" or "straight life".			X		
3. Offers only a pure death benefit with no cash value buildup.	X				
4. Invests the cash value that accumulates into variable mutual fund subaccounts that invest in stocks, bonds, cash, and real estate.		X			
5. This is one of the most popular forms of cash-value life insurance in the marketplace today and has three basic subcategories.					X
6. It contains a savings account that accumulates cash value on a tax-deferred basis, and at least a portion of this money can usually be accessed at any time by the policy owner with no tax consequences and can be used for any purpose.				X	
7. It only remains in force for a predetermined period, such as 10 or 20 years.	X				
8. Pays the policy owner dividends periodically, such			X		

as quarterly or annually, which are based on a guaranteed interest rate.					

Activity 5 - Which of the following is not a recommended strategy for business owners to protect themselves and their assets in case of divorce?

Review your options for establishing a buy-sell agreement, corporation, LLC, or living trust to restrict ownership and ownership transfer.
Revise your partnership agreement to require that the other partners have the option to buy out the interests of the divorced partner and his or her spouse.
Carefully establish, fund, and manage your business with separate assets.
Avoid co-mingling business assets with personal assets and business accounts with personal accounts.
Build up your company enough to the point that you are satisfied, and then try to sell.
Pay yourself a market-rate salary.
If a business is at issue in the divorce, a value must be placed on it. Agree on a number you both can live with. Then consider how to distribute it to your spouse by cash payment, by an offset against other assets you will waive, or with installment payments.

Activity 6: Choose which option best reflects the action's impact on the business's value.

Select the impact on the business value	Increases	Decreases	It Depends
1. Reducing reliance on a single customer.	X		
2. Focusing only on revenue.			X
3. Increasing reliance on a single employee.		X	
4. Increasing reliance on a single supplier.		X	
5. Focusing on selling less stuff to more people.			X
6. Creating recurring revenue.	X		
7. Moving your business to a better location with physical characteristics that are difficult to replicate.	X		
8. Having a customer that amounts to more than 20% of your revenue.			X
9. Creating a unique product or service that is difficult to replicate.	X		
10. Not having audited statements.		X	
11. Creating predictable customer conversion rates.	X		
12. Having all the knowledge and power of the business in the hands of the owner.		X	
13. Not having a platform for customers to review products and services.			X
14. Increasing profits.	X		
15. Developing a brand.	X		

Activity 7: Select True or False.

To maximize business value and avoid overestimating your business's value, you should...	T / F
1. Separate yourself from emotional attachment to the business.	T
2. Set up your business so it is reliant on you.	F
3. Sell hard assets like real estate.	F
4. Understand how business valuation works.	T
5. Develop relationships with potential buyers over time.	T
6. Show income or profitability.	T
7. Maintain a constant business size without scaling up.	F
8. Develop a strong and recognizable brand that drives repeat business.	T

CHAPTERS 8, 9, 10, and 11 - ANSWER KEY

Activity 1: Select True or False.

Questions	T/F
1. It is easier for a business owner to assess their own business objectively without external help.	F
2. A business assessment should focus only on financial performance.	F
3. Knowing your starting point and destination is critical for business success.	T
4. Envisioning should include short-term, medium-term, and long-term goals.	T
5. Creating a vision means drafting a simple vision statement.	F
6. Financial analysis is optional when planning business growth.	F
7. To develop an optimized business model, you must know your gross and net profits.	T
8. Marketing analysis includes studying your competition.	T
9. Fixed costs have no impact on business profitability.	F
10. Implementation plans must define roles and responsibilities.	T
11. Tracking performance is optional if you trust your employees.	F
12. All initiatives should be rolled out simultaneously to save time.	F
13. Measurement and tracking must include both qualitative and quantitative data.	T
14. The SBPro Methodology is a one-time process.	F

Activity 2: Multiple Choice Questions

1. According to the workbook, which aspect is NOT essential when envisioning your business?

   - **C) Color schemes of your office**

2. Why is external input often required during an assessment?

   - **B) To provide a more objective perspective**

3. When should you reevaluate your vision?

   - **B) Annually**

4. Which is NOT a way to optimize your variable costs?

   - **C) Outsource non-core services**

5. When creating recommendations, how many key initiatives should you focus on?

   - **A) 1 to 3**

6. Which of these is NOT part of successful implementation?

   - **C) No need for measurements**

7. What is the final phase of the SBPro Methodology?

   - **B) Implementation & Tracking**

8. What kind of mindset should you maintain when tracking results?

   - **C) Proactive**

Author Bio

ANDREW FRAZIER, MBA, CFA
"The Masterpreneur" and Founder
Small Business Pro University
Andrew@MySBPro.com

Andrew Frazier, MBA, CFA, Masterpreneur™, and founder of Small Business Pro University, is revolutionizing how business owners scale. Through his groundbreaking Masterpreneur™ Playbook Framework, Andrew helps entrepreneurs unlock their leadership potential and drive rapid, sustainable growth.

With over 15 years of experience as a business coach, consultant, and trainer, Andrew has worked 1-on-1 with over 1,000 business owners, identifying the key challenges that prevent them from reaching their goals. His Masterpreneur™ Playbook Framework addresses critical knowledge gaps and skill deficiencies, offering a proven methodology that empowers business owners in any industry to lead confidently and achieve extraordinary results.

His unique, holistic approach combines business strategy, financial expertise, and leadership coaching to help entrepreneurs make data-driven decisions, optimize profits, and fuel sustainable growth. As an author of three influential business books, host of the "Leadership LIVE @ 8:05! Talking Small Business" Livestream/podcast with over 200 episodes, and organizer of high-impact business networking events over 12 years, Andrew's influence reaches tens of thousands of business owners, delivering actionable insights and multimillion-dollar results.

Andrew Frazier's journey from a paper route in 4th grade to a renowned business leader is a testament to his relentless drive and unmatched expertise. Andrew has developed a unique ability to guide business owners through complex challenges by combining his MIT Engineering, NYU MBA, and Chartered Financial Analyst (CFA) education with real-world experience as a Naval Officer, Fortune 500 executive, and serial entrepreneur. His diverse background allows him to bring a multifaceted perspective to every client, empowering them to achieve breakthrough results by evolving as leaders and transforming their businesses.

The Most Comprehensive Suite of Content and Resources for Entrepreneurs and Business Owners

www.SBProU.com

Why Join?

Access to valuable content, resources, and relationships to build your business FASTER and EASIER

www.SBProU.com/membership

Test Drive a FREE Course

https://learn.smallbusinessprouniversity.com/

www.ingramcontent.com/pod-product-compliance
Lightning Source LLC
Chambersburg PA
CBHW081820200326
41597CB00023B/4317